PHARRELL WILLIAMS

BLURRING THE LINES

PHARRELL WILLIAMS

BLURRING THE LINES

CHRIS ROBERTS

CARLTON
BOOKS

This is a Carlton Book

This edition published in 2016 by
Carlton Books Limited
20 Mortimer Street
London W1T 3JW

ISBN 978-1-78097-652-5

1 3 5 7 9 10 8 6 4 2

Printed in China

CONTENTS

INTRODUCTION

"There's something magical about a rhythm you've never heard before. No matter where you are, whatever galaxy, where there's life there's movement. And where there's movement, there's sound. And where there's sound, there's music." Thus philosophised Pharrell Williams, addressing the Oxford Union, Oxford University, as a guest speaker in November 2004.

Almost exactly ten years on, in late 2014, Pharrell was honoured for that music with a star on the Hollywood Walk Of Fame. Attending the ceremony accompanied by his wife Helen and their six-year-old son Rocket, he sported a big hat (of course), a Red Hot Chili Peppers T-shirt, several necklaces and a pair of red Chanel boots bearing the slogan: "Don't same the world – Change." A few days later, Pharrell's 'Happy' was declared the biggest selling single of the year.

He's a solid-gold hit machine and a smart businessman but eight-time Grammy winner Pharrell Williams is also, he has said, a synesthete. Synesthesia is a neurological phenomenon in which, loosely, the stimulation of one sense leads to automatic, involuntary experiences in a second sense. In some cases, letters or numbers are seen as colours or perceived as smells; music too can be heard "in colour". "It's just the way I've always seen music," he's said. "It's not a rarity. Most artists have it." Asked in 2014 by the *Daily Telegraph's* Craig McLean to elaborate on what colours he'd describe his mega-hits like 'Happy', 'Get Lucky' or 'Blurred Lines' as, he mused: "'Get Lucky' is, like, Renaissance-type colours. And 'Happy' is yellows...and mustards. And slight slivers of orange, with a tinge of brown in the verses. And in the choruses, it's more like sherbet colours. Like bright sherbet orange. Pastel oranges. And blues. It's very rainbow-ish. Because those are minor colours but they're exotic colours, juxtaposed to the sharpness and brightness of the major sensation that's in the verses."

Clearly, Pharrell has given this some thought. He remains by all accounts an enigmatic interviewee, prone to pausing lengthily between almost Zen-like utterances, and avoiding any discussion of his private life. In recent years his music has done the talking, the aforementioned global pop anthems breaking records and establishing him as the go-to guru of modern chart magic. Prior to that his track record, both as producer and artist with The Neptunes and N*E*R*D., was dazzling, diverse and matchlessly influential. Now he's using more than his ears, employing his senses in a range of activities. His multi-media venture encompasses fashion, music, art and entertainment under the umbrella name I am OTHER. He owns such brands as Billionaire Boys Club, ICECREAM, Billionaire Girls Club, Bionic Yarn and his own YouTube channel. He's designed jewellery, a fragrance, furniture, sunglasses and sculpture. He's scored blockbuster films, curated prestigious art shows and is building an after-school centre in his hometown Virginia Beach. He's a coach on the American TV show *The Voice*. He's regularly top of Best-Dressed Man polls. He's a businessman and a "universalist". It's telling that he's fond of the word "Renaissance".

All those senses are being actively deployed.

It can often feel like it's Pharrell Williams's world and the rest of us just live in it, envying his cheekbones and eternal youthful looks. It's the music, however, which put Pharrell on top of this world. With

Chad Hugo, The Neptunes hit on the worldwide R&B-pop sound of the Noughties and onwards, working with Kelis, Britney Spears, Busta Rhymes, Daft Punk, Jay Z, Justin Timberlake, Nelly, Snoop Dogg, Beyoncé, Gwen Stefani, Usher, Mariah Carey, John Legend, Madonna, Shakira and countless others. Superstar or wannabe, you had to have a Neptunes link or you had no hit and no credibility. Radio stations were dominated by Neptunes productions, remixes and cameo appearances.

Their slinky, mechanized beats both expanded and wilfully contracted the sound of hip-hop and pop in the late 90s and early 00s. From 'I'm A Slave For You' to 'Rock Your Body', they bossed it. They brought the vibe. Pharrell's own hit 'Frontin'' showcased his kooky wordplay and feathery falsetto.

Then just as it seemed the brand name might have run its course, with the passing of the decade, Pharrell ingeniously rebooted, as himself, or a version of himself. A tall Vivienne Westwood Buffalo hat and he had a much-discussed new image. Now a married father, his collaborations were expertly gauged, as Daft Punk's infectious 'Get Lucky' and Robin Thicke's (controversial, maybe not so expertly gauged) 'Blurred Lines' became the biggest sellers of an era. Both were million-sellers – in the same month. Even these were surpassed by the ubiquity of 'Happy', a song commissioned for the movie *Despicable Me 2*, which broke free of its moorings and launched the Williams persona into the commercial stratosphere. The insanely catchy, upbeat song became a cause célèbre, its joie de vivre transcending language across the planet. Now he could even forge a career-transforming hit for Ed Sheeran.

Back in 2003, a survey suggested that a staggering 43 per cent of the contemporary songs played on American radio stations were The Neptunes' productions. And on UK radio, it was an impressive 20 per cent. You wouldn't think you could top that, but with his triple-whammy of lucky-blurred-happy million-selling hits, Oscar-nominated, multiple Grammy-winner Pharrell now has. To date, he's sold over 50 million singles and 20 million albums.

So how did the man with the Midas touch climb the mountain? Where did he come from, and where is he going to next? Let's look back at his youth, at the fateful, youthful meetings with Chad and with Teddy Riley. The music that inspired them. The reinventions that The Neptunes skilfully grafted on to big-name acts. The hits and the N*E*R*D. project, in which the pair detoured in search of heavier rap-rock. The associations with the big-league players; the solo projects that arguably surpassed those of his idols. The concepts behind his albums *In My Mind* and *G I R L*. All the extra-curricular ventures which have made Pharrell a frontin' mogul and revered songwriter. From getting fired from a job at McDonalds to crying on *The Oprah Winfrey Show* at witnessing how his music moved the world, Pharrell has lived an extraordinary life, making extraordinary sounds. A room without a roof, up all night to the sun. No wonder he's happy.

CHAPTER 1
RHYTHM AND ROOTS

"You have to understand that the world I grew up in was not one of high expectations," Pharrell told an audience of students in 2004. "No-one told us when we were young to be ambitious. In Virginia, if you didn't die in your twenties, you'd probably end up in prison, or live a life of drugs. I feel so privileged that I've been blessed by God.
I feel mega, mega fortunate."

Pharrell was born on 5 April 1973, in Virginia Beach, Virginia. He is the oldest – by a distance – of the three sons of Pharaoh Williams, a handyman, and Carolyn, an elementary school teacher. His brothers are Cato (ten years younger, a keen skateboarder) and Psolomon (twenty years younger). He also has two half-brothers, Pharaoh and David.

In the area where he grew up, it was generally perceived that kids could not even dream of a successful future. More young men joined gangs than went to college; many were, as Pharrell has said, victims of gang-related violence. But Pharrell has also emphasised the positives of growing up in the South. Music was there for him from a young age. And when his family moved from the inner-city to the (relatively) calmer suburbs, when he was seven, he recalls taking on board the influence of a wide range of musical styles – from Madonna to Genesis. This, he reckons, is where his tendency to mix different styles into fresh patterns came from.

"We lived across the street from a biker group," he told hitz.fm. "They were called The Renegades, and were kind of like Hell's Angels. They played a lot of rock 'n' roll, so they'd be playing 'Born To Be Wild' by Steppenwolf across the street. Meanwhile, in my house, my mom and dad are playing Earth, Wind & Fire. And on the radio, they're playing Rick James, or Queen." Musing on the everyday mash-ups, he muttered, "I never really lost that..."

"It wasn't like third-world poverty," his brother David has recounted. "But let's just say we ate a lot of pork and beans." Virginia was tough, but it gave Williams complex musical roots. And when he met another Virginia Beach native, Chad Hugo, aged twelve, those roots came out to play. Williams and Hugo were at different schools but met on a "music improvisation" program, a form of summer camp or Band Camp, while in the seventh grade. There, Pharrell was playing drums and keyboards, and Hugo the tenor saxophone. They were also, believe it or not, members of a marching band, with Pharrell a snare drummer and Hugo a student conductor. They swiftly bonded over a shared love of music and the recognition of each other's talents.

Although Williams – who had by now acquired the teenage nickname Skateboard P – was at Princess Anne High School (playing in their school band), and Hugo at Kempsville High School, they kept up their friendship. And in the early Nineties they formed a four-piece R&B band with friends Shay Haley (later a key player in N*E*R*D) and Mike Etheridge. They entered a high school talent contest. The name they chose was Nobody Knows. Eventually they renamed the outfit as The Neptunes. It was to prove an enduring friendship (and business partnership), and become a powerful name.

Chad, when the pair were later interviewed by VH1, recalled their very early days. Little did anyone realize what their youthful jams (if you could call them that) would lead to. They would, he said, "bang on the cafeteria tables. Pharrell would freestyle. That developed into making music in my garage after school. Pharrell would come up with hooks and beats. We had the cheapest keyboards ever, like a small Casio. When we started working together, Pharrell would bring to my house records that his parents listened to. So you'd have a loop of some guy singing with all these instruments and orchestration behind it. We'd listen to it over and over again, then turn it off and mix something inspired by its sound. That's not a formula. We just did that."

On a *CBS News* interview in April 2014, Pharrell clarified that there was a popular "misconception". He didn't meet Chad in "band camp", but "connected with him" in "beginning band class": a significant distinction in American school culture, apparently. "I lived in the Salem area," he explained, "and we were actually able to attend the Kemps Landing district. It was pretty weird how that worked"

"So, we'd see each other at band camp, and sometimes I would go to his house to play. Because he had Casio keyboards, and we would make little tracks. Just for fun! And then I met Shay, who's also in N*E*R*D. Sometimes I'd bring him over to Chad's house with me when we'd make music, and we just ended up having this little band. And that's when we started entering high school contests – because we loved the music that we were making, and we wanted to show people what we were doing. I mean, we didn't think it was going to end up here, like, doing an interview with you, come on!"

Chad Hugo has on various other occasions recalled the young pair's coming together. In an interview with *HK Magazine* as he prepared to DJ in Hong Kong, he was asked how they first formed as a unit. "I had an interest in electronic music," Hugo mused. "We were enrolled in a school for the arts in sixth grade, where we learned how to sequence. We took part in jazz-fusion songs, and in our free time we learned how to program beats. One of the teachers had an argument that turntable scratching wasn't an art form, and Pharrell always argued that it was. There was one teacher who agreed with us! We said, 'We like that D.J. stuff', and so we got together after school and made beats. Pharrell would ride his Honda scooter to my place. It was a way to learn more about music, and it was fun. It was kind of like video games for us! I saved up some money for a sequential multi-track: my mom helped me out. I didn't know what it was, but it sounded cool. It was a great way to try something new." Chad has also previously said, "Have you seen that Jack Black movie *School Of Rock*? That was us, except we played jazz standards like Herbie Hancock's 'Watermelon Man.'"

The Neptunes simply added a third member when they wished to metamorphose into N*E*R* D. "Shay came by later on," recalled Hugo. (Shay is also known as "Shae" or "Shade".) "At first, as a dancer. I remember Pharrell was talking to rapper-D.J. Biz Markie, and he said Biz wanted tracks. At first I didn't believe him. At that time, Pharrell sounded like Rakim, of Eric B. and Rakim (the legendary hip-hop duo). And one of my favourite songs was their (1988 hit) 'Follow The

Leader'. Pharrell was like a hippie Rakim, only if Rakim had an afro and wore bell-bottoms! Anyway we did well, we made some jams."

Chad may be the least high-profile of the pair now, but a little background on the man described by *Source* magazine as the "Mr Spock to Pharrell's Captain Kirk" (a comparison he disliked, saying he's not "stiff" like *Star Trek's* Spock) is essential. Born 24 February 1974, he's a saxophonist, pianist, and guitarist as well as the genius sequencer behind The Neptunes. Though born in South Hampton Roads, a city in Portsmouth, Virginia, he grew up in Virginia Beach. His parents were Filipino: his father was a retired Navy officer, his mother was a laboratory technician.

Now Chad and Pharrell were about to experience a huge stroke of life-changing good fortune. Red-hot producer Teddy Riley elected to open his new studio, Future Records, right next door to the school in Virginia Beach. He'd made his name working with Bobby Brown, Al B. Sure, Keith Sweat and others, earning a reputation as the progenitor of the funky and fashionable New Jack Swing genre. Of course, his biggest major-league triumph was, famously, producing half of mega-star Michael Jackson's *Dangerous* album, having been recommended to the musician by no less a figure in Jackson's musical career than Quincy Jones. He was responsible for the hits 'Remember The Time', 'Jam' and 'In The Closet'. The album sold 32 million copies. Based in Virginia from the early Nineties, as well as discovering The Neptunes he was at that time the force behind

Blackstreet and producing such various talents as Melanie B (of the Spice Girls), Boys II Men and Snoop Dogg.

And as Riley was producing the second Wreckx-N-Effect album, *Hard Or Smooth*, he got The Neptunes involved. They assisted on 'Rump Shaker', which turned out to be a huge 1992 hit single. But let's not jump ahead of ourselves.

Around the same time as Riley opened his studio, the eagerly inventive young Pharrell and Chad had formed a side-group, a hip-hop and production trio, which they named SBI, standing for Surrounded By Idiots. The third member of their trio was none other than Timbaland. Today, of course, just like the other two (and indeed Riley), Timbaland enjoys a status as one of the most successful and influential producers and hit-makers in the world. (They disbanded before recording, and Timbaland & Magoo became a friendly rival duo.) Among Timbaland's most famous music now is his work with Missy Elliott, Aaliyah, Nelly Furtado, Rihanna, Drake, Jay Z, and Justin Timberlake. "Timbaland is a genius; I still look up to him to this day," Pharrell told Ian Gittins of *Man About Town* magazine in 2010.

At this early stage, in his late teens, Pharrell dreamed of being a soul singer. "Yes sir!" he told Gittins. "That was the dream back then. But then I started writing songs, and producing them, and I realized I could love that just as much." And did he imagine he'd have such mind-blowing success? "Not at all! When I was growing up, doing something like this never seemed like a possibility. It wasn't even on my wish list. I just figured I'd study my ass off and try to be some kind of art professor. But this happened instead – and I am grateful."

Talent shows get a lot of criticism since the manipulation of *The X Factor*, but without one we may not have seen the successful Pharrell – now of course a coach on the American version of *The Voice* – that we know today. Because it was at a high-school talent show that Teddy Riley just happened to attend that he spotted Hugo and Williams performing. He enlisted Pharrell to write some lyrics, and the result was the rap verse of 'Rump Shaker'. Thus, Pharrell's first professional work in the music industry was more successful than many other artists manage in a lifetime, as the single went double platinum.

Pharrell had his big break. After that he and Hugo had offers coming in to write, mix and create backing beats, as well as opportunities to sing backing vocals. But The Neptunes were not yet firing on all cylinders, and remained a good distance away from their real, big-league breakthrough. They still struggled to get traction lifting themselves to the next level. Their image – or lack of one – was proving something of a problem.

After graduating from high school, the pair signed with Teddy Riley as The Neptunes. In 1994 they assisted with the production of the track 'Tonight's The Night' from Riley's band Blackstreet's eponymous debut. There were occasional bright moments after that, but not the swift leap into the spotlight they'd hoped for.

That non-image may have held them back. It may have been a blessing in disguise, as they honed their skills. Chad Hugo told VH1 years later that they were frequently told they didn't have the right look for the highly fashion-conscious hip-hop industry. The young duo resisted faking it, being focused on their musical learning curve. They wouldn't be deterred from working the way they saw fit.

Said a self-deprecating Hugo, "You have people who are like: 'Who are these nerdy dudes?' At the end of the day, your music speaks for itself. Three years ago, when we did a video, I had on, like, cowboy boots, regular jeans, and a polo shirt. My hair was big and matted, and I didn't care. I had people thinking I was an engineer. When we would walk into the studio they would be asking me where to order the best pizza. I was like: 'Dog, I don't know, man. Let me fix up this track for you here.' And I guess they're not used to seeing an Asian making music. But I'm just here to get people's heads bobbing..."

The Neptunes were not far away from getting a whole multitude of heads bobbing. Their kaleidoscopic ascent was highly imminent.

CHAPTER 2
THE BREAKTHROUGH

As they strove to capture the magic formula that would lift them to stratospheric heights of hipness, Pharrell and Hugo paid attention to what was going on in Riley's studio, listening and learning. At this stage, Pharrell was still shaking off the nickname Skateboard P, given to him in his early teens at Princess Anne High School. His brother Cato is a professional skater, while Pharrell remains a keen fan. "The first sport I got into – and the one that has had the most impact on my life – is skateboarding," he has said. "Most people think skateboarding is for some kid with blond hair from suburbia. But I remember when I was twelve or thirteen, growing up in Virginia Beach, everybody – black and white – was doing it." He went further. "Skating taught me what it meant to be cool, to have credibility. I had it. I got so mad about it that I had a half-pipe put in my house. I had the look – the baggy jeans, the Vans. I still wear Vans shoes. I rap about skateboarding."

Perhaps the first elements of The Neptunes' "image" filtered through from those roots. As a rebellious youth Pharrell also went through a heavy tattoo phase, which he later regretted. In an interview years later he expressed a wish to get rid of them and start afresh. "I was just young and dumb," he confessed. "I ended up getting them as fast as I could, just going through a really crazy rebellious period. I got a lot of them." He tried a complicated, strange-sounding tattoo-removal process. "It's basically like getting a skin graft, but you're not taking skin from your ass or your legs. These guys actually grow the skin for you. First you have to give them a sample of your skin, which they then replicate. Once that's been done, they sew it on... and it's seamless." He's also since been through the painful process of laser tattoo removal.

Pharrell was no stranger to typical teenage traumas and problems. Now everybody knows he wrote and produced the ubiquitous McDonalds jingle 'I'm Lovin' It', as sung by Justin Timberlake. Yet he had a history with the burger brand, and a less than entirely happy one at that. He worked at branches of theirs when he was seventeen, presumably for a considerably lower fee than the jingle commanded. And he got fired. Three times. He wasn't yet the workaholic he'd turn out to be, not by a long chalk.

"When I was seventeen I was freshly fired from three separate McDonalds jobs," he's recalled. "I was lazy. I hated mopping the floor, and I hated opening up. Do you know what opening up means? It means you're there at 5 o'clock in the lazy-ass morning. It wasn't fun! Man....my manager at the time, he was like, 'Pharrell, you are costing me a fortune. Clock out.' Because I was burning all the meat too. I never stole anything ever, but at that time I definitely kept a pocket full of chicken nuggets. They were so good! So... I got fired from three different ones."

Clearly, Pharrell's future didn't lie in burger flipping. He and Chad Hugo needed to knuckle down with their music. In 1996, when Pharrell was 23, Teddy Riley got them involved in production on tracks by SWV and Total. If they didn't yet demonstrate any particular trademark style, it was definitely progress.

SWV (aka Sisters With Voices) were a New-York based female R&B trio who enjoyed success throughout the Nineties. (They disbanded in

1998 but reformed in 2005). Major hits included 'Right Here' (which on the better-known, US chart-topping Teddy Riley remix sampled Michael Jackson's 'Human Nature'), 'I'm So Into You', 'Weak' and 'You're The One'. On the UK remix of 'Right Here', Pharrell contributed a short rap. 'Right Here/Human Nature' hung around the American charts for over a year, to the point where SWV admitted they didn't really like what Teddy had done to their debut single. They couldn't complain about its impact however. Pharrell's main claim to fame here was chanting "S... to the double... the U... the V!" It became a catchphrase in the band's shows. He was credited as a co-producer, but bear in mind there were around twenty various mixes of the single as it enjoyed international success, so he wasn't a household name just yet.

Total were a Newark, New Jersey R&B girl trio, signed by Sean Combs's (aka P Diddy) Bad Boy Records. Hits included 'Trippin'' (featuring Missy Elliott), 'Can't You See?' (featuring The Notorious B.I.G.) and 'Kissing You'. Their 1996 self-titled debut album saw Pharrell and Chad (as The Neptunes) credited with co-writing (with the Bee Gees, who'd been sampled) and co-producing (with Sean "Puffy" Combs) the track 'When Boy Meets Girl'. (The full number of producers on the album ran into double figures.)

By the time of their involvement with the Mase album *Harlem World*, the following year, The Neptunes were starting to define their style. Another Bad Boy artist discovered by Puffy, Mase had made high-profile guest rap spots on tracks by everyone from Keith Sweat to Mariah Carey, and featured on Puff Daddy's own hits. His own solo debut established him as a name in his own right. Puff Daddy promoted him as his label's premier act. *Harlem World* went straight in at number one on the Billboard pop and R&B charts, selling over a quarter of a million copies in the U.S. its first week on release. It later qualified as a four-times-platinum album. Singles 'Feel So Good' and 'What You Want' were enormous hits, and preceded 'Lookin' At Me', which was equally big in '98 – and produced by The Neptunes.

Mase, interviewed on MTV, displayed impressive talking-about-self-in-third-person tendencies, saying, "I'm trying to establish a strong identity and foundation for Mase so a lot of people could know that Mase is his own person and Mase can do other things besides rap and music and things in that nature." *Entertainment Weekly's* reviewer praised the album's "creatively refreshing, well-crafted lyrics... rap's newest bad boy more than holds his own. His distinctive marble-mouthed drawl creates a regular-guy persona all too rare in hip-hop."

Yet if Mase was trying to prove he was his own person, he had a lot of helpers. Elite hip-hop artists like Busta Rhymes, Jay-Z, Lil' Kim, Total and DMX all contributed, Combs shared production credits with Jermaine Dupri, Stevie J, D-Dot... and the then-unknown The Neptunes. 'Lookin' At Me', their offering, featured Puff Daddy himself and brought home a gold disc. Williams and Hugo's name was beginning to get around. "Puff is still one of my heroes," Pharrell has said. "And Mase, he had the golden voice, no-one was touching that. It was a moment for us, because those were our heroes."

In September 1998 came the release of a hit that solidified their growing reputation. Noreaga's 'Superthug' reached number one on the Hot Rap Tracks chart, and edged into the top forty on the Billboard Hot 100. The Puerto Rican American rapper's debut solo album *N.O.R.E.* eventually went gold, and featured guest spots by Busta Rhymes, Nas, Mase and Jadakiss. Formerly half of the hardcore rap duo Capone-N-Noreaga, Victor "Noreaga" Santiago Jr. had met his rap partner while both were in prison, but went solo when Kiam "Capone" Holley was sent back to jail after violating the terms of his parole. 'Superthug', on the Tommy Boy label, alerted the music business to the fact that The Neptunes were now very much happening, and kick-started their climb to Billboard's "Producer Of The Decade" of the 2000s. Incidentally, Janet Jackson later sampled it for the track 'Ruff (I Like It)', also produced by The Neptunes, but strangely the cut never made it onto one of her albums.

By then, it didn't much matter: The Neptunes were flying. At the tail end of 1999 came the release of the full album that proved, as producers, they could deliver. Kelis's debut album *Kaleidoscope*, emerging on 7 December, suggested loud and clear that Williams and Hugo were the men sculpting the sound of the next decade.

It had been trailered by its extraordinary lead single, 'Caught Out There'. Although this song peaked at number 55 in the US, it became

Kelis's breakthrough top five hit in the UK (and the Netherlands). And Kelis nearly didn't get to sing it, or wouldn't have if one of Pharrell's idols, Busta Rhymes, hadn't considered it unimpressive.

"I made Kelis's 'Caught Out There' for Busta Rhymes," Pharrell told *Vulture* in an interview, many years on. "I'll never forget. He's my brother. At the time, we sat in an office at Elektra Records, and I played him that beat and I was sure he was going to love it. But he was just, like, reading a sports magazine, listening to these tracks. Still, I was honoured! Because it was Busta. In full pigtail dreads. You don't understand – he was like the king to me. All these people – they were like deities! It was like being on Mount Olympus, where Apollo and the gods were, to be around these people. Think about it – Busta's voice is not ordinary... But here he is! And he's chewing gum, not even looking up one time, but I was so honoured. So... that song went out to be Kelis's..."

Kelis however was, and remains, quite a character, and certainly "not ordinary". "I've always felt like a star," she told me in 2000 as her career roared into life. "Just because you now agree doesn't mean I wasn't one before I had a record deal." I'd reviewed the album in *Uncut* magazine, praising its explosive energy and eccentricity, and hinting that these "The Neptunes" chaps, whoever they might be, with their radical fusion of soul and hip-hop, could be a force to come. "You'll have been introduced by now to the wigged-out world of Kelis, through her debut single 'Caught Out There', with its infectious, hollered refrain of 'I hate you so much right now!'" I wrote. "It's already ensconced as one of the year's best, a feminist 'No Diggity', the kind of thing which Missy Elliott, for all the hype and costly videos, has singularly failed to approach."

Gender politics was, thankfully, just one string to the precocious teenager's bow. "This album," I continued, "prompting the steamiest word-of-mouth since Macy Gray, is a stunning collision/collusion of hip-hop, soul and swing, raiding random decades, street-smart but ghetto fabulous. It's pop enough to crossover.... (but) sassy enough for its core audience, who'll know the previous work of producers The Neptunes (Mase, Blackstreet, SWV). It could prove the biggest breakthrough since The Fugees's *The Score*. Harlem universe-trotter Kelis appeared on Ol' Dirty Bastard's 'Got Your Money', but *Kaleidoscope* is less of a flash in a pan than a storm in a dustbowl. As hip-hop stalls and 'soul' sinks into sterile self-parody, this – with sublime arrogance – seizes the reins and makes a decision. (Prince will hear this and weep. Or, if he's still hungry to get it back, be inspired."

My enthusiasm was tempered for the then-topical "irksome spoken comedy" punctuations and "cosmic" gobbledegook, but the grooves won me back. "'Good Stuff' brings us in with an irresistible bass groove, a house piano surge and a chorus of fly girls. The hit follows: in its full incarnation you'll appreciate the beat-perfect juxtaposition of 'babe, I love you' with 'yeah – he's lyin''... and more hooks than a curtain rail."

The album (and production) continued to pop. "On the delicious, erotic 'Mafia', Kelis gets onto the tough stuff, as if we'd lose focus if she didn't drop a few guns in. It's truly seductive, sirens wailing, rhythm insatiable, a sitar in there somewhere. Kelis's superb voice raps, 'While I'm behind you, The Feds won't find you', then sings, 'For you I'd testify' (lending the phrase new meaning). She consistently reinvents old-school soul's sentimental trademarks, and hot-wires them for a more cynical now. 'Suspended' hovers over a dream of bliss, although the rapper whispering 'wake up bitch', with increasing desperation, confuses matters. 'Mars', a barrage, concludes 'Earth to your brain... you're f***ed', after several gags about 'blunt', the likes of which Grammy-darling Lauryn Hill has been striking off her C.V. for years. There's a sumptuous Curtis Mayfield flow to 'Ghetto Children', a taut-as-catgut groove to 'I Want Your Love', and a happy Seventies disco glow to 'Roller Rink', where, in one of the century's best cheap rhymes, there's 'no need for a shrink'.

"There are more peak moments here than on a dozen equally-touted New Saviours Of Black Music releases. (It's)... the real deal. Kelis and her music have class, lack of class, talent and talons. 'All I wanna do is be a serious superstar', she deadpans, early on in this euphoric, elastic extravaganza. She's there." Of course, Pharrell may have been covertly expressing a few of his own subliminal desires in some of the lyrics.

Kelis went on to be nominated for two Grammy Awards, record six studio albums, write a cookbook and develop her own brand of cooking sauces. The *Kaleidoscope* album went gold in the UK and won her a Brit Award as International Breakthrough Act. She'd reunite with The Neptunes for her 2001 follow-up, *Wanderland.* American success however was at this stage limited, which must have frustrated The Neptunes somewhat. They'd recorded the album in Virginia Beach at Master Sound studios. Pharrell guested on some tracks; 'Ghetto Children' even credited N*E*R*D. as backing vocalists. Some critics had viewed *Kaleidoscope* as veering insufficiently from the mainstream, from not following through on its early promises. The Neptunes still had a little distance to cover before they'd defined the sound of the new century.

That new century was also, of course, to see the rise to world domination of rapper Jay-Z. He was already well in the ascendant, established as a towering figure in the field, when the single 'I Just Wanna Love U (Give It 2 Me)', released on the last day of October in 2000, gave him one of his biggest hits to date, nudging the top ten on the Billboard Hot 100. Taken from his fifth studio album *The Dynasty: Roc La Familia*, which debuted at number one and has now sold more than two-and-a-half million copies (including over half a million in its first week), it was a hugely important production credit for The Neptunes. It also gave Pharrell a "featuring" nod. (The album was rated one of the highest R&B/hip-hop sellers of the subsequent decade.)

Pharrell sang on the chorus, as did Shay Haley and Omillio Sparks. This chorus was taken from the 1981 Rick James song 'Give It To Me

Baby', which had topped the chart itself in its day, and has become something of a favourite for samplers, appearing in various forms in Michael Jackson's 'Thriller', MC Hammer's 'Let's Get It Started', Public Enemy's 'Fight The Power' and 'P&P 1.5' by Kendrick Lamar. Janet Jackson and Coldplay have since used the Jay-Z track at some of their live concerts, as pre-show music. The track credits no less than ten writers, including Shawn Carter (Jay-Z), Sean Combs, Pharrell and Chad Hugo, but The Neptunes were sole producers. Even within the lyric, Jay-Z hailed "the Neptunes sound". Said Pharrell, who has collaborated with Jay-Z regularly ever since, "He just continues to get better, like fine wine. He's something else. When you talk to him, you see purple. He's wisdom."

Jay-Z declared (on Bill Maher's TV show, *Real Time*) that the song was based on a true story, after events that took place at a Mary J. Blige after-show party. Britney Spears found it so fun and playful that she decided there and then she wanted to work with The Neptunes. "For this album (*Britney*) I was really inspired by Jay-Z and The Neptunes," she said. "Those were the two people I really listened to." And by the next year 'I'm A Slave 4 U' was to become a watershed moment in the careers of both the pop starlet and The Neptunes themselves. But the boys weren't done with shaking up the dancefloors of 2000 yet.

CHAPTER 3
TWENTY-FIRST CENTURY SOUND

In the last months of the twentieth century, Pharrell and Chad, as The Neptunes, had collaborated with increasingly high-profile names, from Clipse to Ol' Dirty Bastard, and even remixed Prince's 'The Greatest Romance Ever Sold'. With the plaudits received for the Kelis debut and the success of the Jay-Z single, they sensed their time was approaching. They seized the day.

Offers for remixes came in thick and fast, and in the year 2000 the pair sprinkled their magic dust over tracks by a broad range of artists, including 504 Boys, All Saints, Angie Stone, Backstreet Boys, Beenie Man, Ludacris and TQ. Often, Pharrell would contribute a rap or vocal part, earning an extra "featuring Pharrell" credit and cannily getting his name around even more. The Neptunes even remixed a Sade track ('By Your Side') and a Rage Against The Machine number (though that didn't make the cut for the rock band's album).

Their biggest number of the year though, apart from the Jay-Z smash, was their huge hit for Mystikal, the distinctly cheeky (and lewd) 'Shake Ya Ass'. Released on 18 July, it won heavy airplay (as did its video). Pharrell, naturally, sang on it. If the title was too risqué for some radio stations, there was an edited "clean" version, named 'Shake It Fast'. That opening line was certainly too raunchy for some.

Mystikal was at first reluctant to release the song, claiming that its light-hearted celebration of a certain part of the human anatomy didn't accurately reflect his abilities "as an artist". Later he acknowledged that its popularity "proved me wrong" and that it was the "biggest song of my career". Years on, the hipper-than-thou US music website *Pitchfork* listed it as the 303rd (no less!) best song of the 2000s. It's appeared in a diverse stream of movies, ads and TV shows, from *Scary Movie 2* to *About A Boy* to *Treme* to *Grand Theft Auto 4* (where it soundtracks a strip club scene).

New Orleans rapper Mystikal (real name Michael Tyler) enjoyed further hits like 'Danger (Been So Long)' but was disgraced in 2004 when sentenced to six years in prison for sexual battery and extortion. In December 2000 though, all involved were jubilant as 'Danger' – another Neptunes construction – almost matched the chart figures of 'Shake Ya Ass'. They'd also produced 'Jump' and 'Family' for the album, *Let's Get Ready*, from which the hits emerged. *Let's Get Ready* leaped to number one, going double platinum in the US. *Entertainment Weekly* called Mystikal "the James Brown of hip-hop". While it labelled 'Shake Ya Ass' as "crass" it reckoned 'Danger (Been So Long)' "contrasts the rapper's rasp with gentle Eastern instrumentation". AllMusic also noted the James Brown references in "Shake Ya Ass", saying that this "blazing" lead single was "exploding with more exuberance and energy than humans are supposed to have". It remarked that The Neptunes' "sparse funk" and "odd sounds" "just sound straight-up funky".

And as The Neptunes produced bigger and bigger hits, Pharrell got noticed. His singing on some of the tracks – first as background vocalist, then performing choruses – led to him appearing in the stars' videos. His smooth voice, good looks and quiet but confident demeanour spoke of a subtle, slow-burning charisma. He was beginning to get his own fans, despite having never released a record or played a gig under his own name.

But then, oops... they did it again. Britney Spears was still (just) a teenager in September 2001 when 'I'm A Slave 4 U' emerged. "By the time of this single (the first song from her third album), it was obvious Britney Spears was becoming an adult," wrote About.com. "This song is a radical shift from the 'not quite innocent' 16-year-old schoolgirl of her first album. Slinky and sexy have crept into the Britney style." "I'm not a girl, not yet a woman", Spears famously sang on another track. The Neptunes helped Britney graduate to the latter role.

Born in McComb, Mississippi in 1981, Britney had already graduated from The Mickey Mouse Club when 'Baby One More Time' and 'Oops!... I Did It Again' rocketed her to global fame. The former, one of the best-selling singles of all time, led to the biggest-selling album ever by a teenage artist. (The record company hadn't fancied it as a single: Britney argued the case, and suggested the "Catholic schoolgirl" video.) The latter led a second album that broke sales records in its first week, debuting at number one. Her tours grossed huge figures. She was a veritable overnight sensation.

Soon she was pushing for more freedom of expression, even keener perhaps than her record company to play up her sexuality. A suggestive, scantily clad 1999 photo shoot for *Rolling Stone* saw the American Family Association calling to "God-loving Americans to boycott stores selling Britney's albums". She retorted, "What's the big deal? I have strong morals. I'd do it again. I thought the pictures were fine. And I was tired of being compared to Debbie Gibson and all this bubblegum pop all the time." Her "racy" onstage outfits also attracted flak and publicity. In February 2001 she landed an eight-million dollar promotional deal with Pepsi.

So her third album *Britney* came out in November that year, carrying high expectations. She demanded a more grown-up, funkier sound. On tour, she'd been listening to hip-hop and R&B, declaring a love for The Neptunes' productions. The album, with Pharrell and Chad busily involved, sold over twelve million worldwide, gained two Grammy nominations, and was the record where, as AllMusic put it, "she strives to deepen her persona, making it more adult while still recognisably Britney. It sounds like the work of a star who has found and refined her voice, resulting in her best record yet." 'I'm A Slave 4 U' was a top ten hit across the planet.

The Neptunes had originally penned the track for Janet Jackson's *All For You* album (as was 'Boys', another track ultimately nabbed by Spears despite Jackson recording a demo), but the link-up with Britney came about through a string of starry connections. Through knowing Jay-Z, Pharrell met fast-rising pop star Justin Timberlake: a meeting that was in itself to lead to great things a year on (which we will, of course, get to). For now though, Timberlake introduced Pharrell to his then-girlfriend, Britney. (Timberlake and Spears were the hot-gossip celebrity couple of the day). Said Pharrell, "Jay-Z introduced me to him (Justin) at a club in New York. He was there with a couple of guys from (his boy band) *NSYNC. Jay was like: 'You have to meet this guy Justin Timberlake.' I was like: 'Oh OK, cool.' Jay was like: 'Y'all need to work together.' And I was like: 'Yeah. Sure.' So we met up and we did 'Girlfriend' (the *NSYNC hit). The funny thing is the song's called 'Girlfriend' and Justin is like, 'I want you to work with my girl.' I said, 'All right, cool.' So he set it up and we did like two songs. You know, we thought it was interesting, but I remember people going, 'Oh, you shouldn't do that. You shouldn't work with people in pop.'"

Here, Pharrell made a decision that was to ensure he expanded his burgeoning production empire and send him from high-cred niche to high-profile supernova. "And I was like: 'Man, we have to have way more vision than that, and we have to be open to other types of creativity, and what that may bring. If you're just closed-minded, and you think categorical all the time, then you're going to be a categorical producer, and I didn't want to do that.'"

When 'I'm A Slave 4 U' came out, some critics remarked on its similarities to Vanity 6's Prince-infused 1982 hit 'Nasty Girl'. Others said Britney's vocals sounded "unnatural". It reached the top ten almost everywhere on the planet, but didn't rise as high as Britney's previous hits. In a way this was a calculated gamble, as she and her "people" knew they had to sacrifice some short-term sales to extend her career, moving into the more grown-up sound. The video, by Francis Lawrence, also veered more adult, featuring Spears dancing (with adoring men) in a sauna. Sometimes belly-dancing. She performed the track regularly in concerts, but its first appearance at the 2001 MTV Music Video Awards in New York drew criticism from PETA (the animal rights group) for her use of exotic animals (like a caged white tiger) as props. A live albino Burmese Python draped around her shoulders guaranteed Britney front-page publicity everywhere. She also opened the 2001 Billboard Music Awards in Las Vegas with the song, memorably performing from a stage set within the fountains of the Bellagio Hotel.

The song's sparse electronica and skittering beats were typical of what was now The Neptunes' trademark sound, recorded at Master Sound in their hometown of Virginia Beach (and later mixed by Serban Ghenea in New York). Of the lusty lyrics and breathy moans and sighs (also fast becoming a Neptunes trademark), Britney said, "It talks about me just wanting to go out and forget who I am, and dance, and have a good time. That's kinda where I am right now. I love working, but at the same time I love having a good time." *NME* magazine described the results as "funk the way God intended – hypnotic, insistent, mysterious, suggestive. And if Prince was a 19-year-old former Disney Club host and virgin, he'd be proud to create such a record." Similarly, another review observed that, "Spears' main musical and visual influence has been not Madonna but Janet Jackson. But Jackson's not the only influence to appear on 'Slave': The Neptunes' minimal, electronic production and Spears' breathy, cooing delivery create a track that smacks of Prince. Spears becomes more and more interesting and enjoyable as she explores these elements..."

All K Pop reckoned that 'Slave' was "a huge step away from the bouncy pop that made her a superstar, in an attempt to leave behind her pigtails and chirpy image, (it) did not suit her style: the vocals were forced and the Janet Jackson slinkiness was unnatural." Most however, like Yahoo! Music, considered it "a real artistic leap". It's perhaps not unrelated that, overall, the single fared better in Europe than in America.

The album, *Britney*, released in November 2001, followed the single's lead in forsaking some sales figures while repositioning her as a more interesting and viable artist. Nonetheless it debuted at number one on the Billboard chart, though its six singles proved to be moderate rather than massive hits. 'I'm A Slave 4 U' was followed by 'Overprotected', 'I'm Not A Girl, Not Yet A Woman', 'I Love Rock 'n' Roll', 'Anticipating' and 'Boys'. The album was Grammy-nominated for Best Pop Vocal Album.

'Boys' was The Neptunes' other offering to the set. (The album's other writer-producers included everyone from Max Martin to Rodney Jerkins to BT to Britney's beau, Timberlake.) It also featured in the Austin Powers movie *Goldmember*. Again, it fared better outside the States (and went gold in Australia). The video featured Britney (promising to "get nasty") and Pharrell (getting his face known again) at a party in a castle, and had cameos from Mike Myers as Austin

Powers, Jason Priestley, DJ Qualls, Taye Diggs and Justin Bruening.

Critics were again mixed in their reactions. "A rap-lite teen-pop tease", said the *Milwaukee Journal Sentinel. Entertainment Weekly* repeated a common refrain: "cut-rate 80s Janet Jackson". What was more important for Pharrell Williams's career here was that the song was (and was perceived as) essentially a duet. And "a decidedly lubricious one", according to the *NME*'s Alex Needham. "She sings about boys, he sings about girls," he continued. "A simple concept, but an effective one, resulting in Britney's best single in ages." The *Yale Daily News* thought it "an envelope-pushing (when you consider her claims of wholesomeness) smut-fest". *Entertainment Weekly* was more intrigued by the sound of it, positing that "(The Neptunes) swaddle her in writhing, kick-the-can beats, but never have a groove and verse been so betrayed by a limp chorus."

Britney still performs the song today, in her Las Vegas residency, *Britney: Piece Of Me*. Shifting from wholesomeness to a "smut-fest" may have moved her stellar career in a radically different direction, but long-term – albeit after a worrying wobble, bordering on a nervous breakdown, and the occasional calamitous marriage – it paid off. "Bad girl" Britney has become more iconic than "Disney princess" Britney. To a large degree she has Pharrell to thank for that.

Pharrell had plenty of other tracks to attend to in 2001. Popular R&B superstar Usher's 'U Don't Have To Call', from his album *8701*, was written by Pharrell alone. Gushed an enthusiastic Pharrell, "He's just a maestro. His voice is unmatched. He supersedes what most people think he can do. I just love when we're able to do colourful black music. There's nothing like that. I love all kinds of music and all genres, but obviously colourful black music is a good feeling for me personally. We were even able to squeeze in two bridges, which is a rarity for pop radio."

The same year, The Neptunes produced parts of the second album by Ray J, *This Ain't A Game*. (This was two years before his sex tape with Kim Kardashian "elevated" him to tragi-comic "star" status. Since then he's endured several bust-ups with the law, and was close to Whitney Houston at the time of her death.) In 2001, he – brother of Brandy Norwood (known as singer Brandy) and first cousin of Snoop Dogg – was a singer with high hopes. The single 'Wait A Minute', featuring Lil Kim and – naturally – Pharrell, was another Neptunes hit. "We just wanted to make something different, something that felt different," recalled Pharrell in an interview. "I was just glad the folks wanted to go there. It's awesome when the people want to go there. It feels like there's a shift right now in music, you know. There's so many really good and brave artists taking chances."

All of which worked just fine for The Neptunes, major movers and shakers now in this new-century shift. 2001, their breakthrough year, also saw sessions or remixes (often featuring Pharrell's voice) with Foxy Brown, P Diddy, T.I., Philly's Most Wanted, *NSYNC (the aforementioned 'Girlfriend', involving Justin Timberlake), Mary J.

Blige, Ludacris, Lil' Bow Wow, Jermaine Dupri, Jadakiss, Babyface and Ice Cube. They were both working and networking. There were even studio sessions/mixes with rock acts like Limp Bizkit, Garbage and Perry Farrell. How they found time to produce two full albums is a miracle, yet they did. The second Kelis album, *Wanderland*, came out in mid-October. Just prior to this, in late September, came the release of the first N*E*R*D album, *In Search Of...*

As they sang there, "everybody is a star". Pharrell and Chad, on top of helping countless other artists refresh and reboot their sound, were about to join the club.

CHAPTER 4
THEIR TIME IS NOW

When Britney had made her much-talked-about, snake-swaddled appearance performing 'I'm A Slave 4 U' at the 2002 MTV Video Music Awards, Pharrell had made a revealing comment to VH1, expressing his pride at watching her sing his song. "It wasn't just about our production," he said. "Those were my lyrics and everything. I didn't care if she flopped at the show. That

was *my* moment. I didn't care if everybody in the place hated it. We made it. Pop-wise, what little girl doesn't know Britney Spears?" It was, for him, confirmation that he'd made it in the music business. He knew the doors were open. For *his* moment.

Britney may have taken The Neptunes' music to a new audience, but the work with Jay-Z, Usher, Kelis, Busta Rhymes and *NSYNC had provided the platform from which they could launch. In 2001, an ambitious Pharrell told an interviewer, "I want you to raise your awareness and listen to this R&B. I tell you, I'm gonna reshape it. I'm gonna get rid of this Range Rover R&B and all this 'platinum' and 'Bentleys' talk. There's so much more to black life and culture than the materialistic portion that seems to consume all the lyrical content on the radio. I want to offer our difference and perspective, and I promise we're gonna make people move – and feel R&B again." He wasn't just blowing smoke: by the end of 2002 The Neptunes had won Producers Of The Year awards at both the Billboard Music Awards and the Source Awards.

Before that, they had broken out of their shell and become recording artists in their own right. Just not as The Neptunes. And not, technically, as an R&B act. Now, curiously, the restless Pharrell and Chad, signed to Virgin by mentor Teddy Riley, decided to reinvent themselves as an alternative rock band. Together with childhood friend Shay Hayley, they formed N*E*R*D. A complete departure. Their "uninhibited" alter ego.

N*E*R*D (an acronym of No-One Ever Really Dies) was conceived as a side-project of The Neptunes' production work for others. Yet so hot was their name (however they veiled it) that their 2001 debut *In Search Of...* sold over 600,000 copies in the States and was certified gold. It also won the second annual Shortlist Music Prize. For the trio, *In Search Of...* was an exploratory journey, which broadened their musical vocabulary.

At first they used similar digital recording techniques to those deployed by The Neptunes, but then felt an urge to sound "different" to the material they'd so far become known for. So after the first version had been released in Europe in September 2001, somewhat overshadowed by the second Kelis album, they felt it needed something more. They re-recorded their album using live instruments, and rock (or power-pop) band Spymob, for a secondary US-targeted release. They dropped the licentious "skits" and "intros". Singles like 'Lapdance' and 'Rock Star' were a startling surprise even to their closest friends and collaborators. The electronic/digital version features drum machines and synthesisers (in conventional Neptunes style), but this rock version is fuelled by thrusting guitars and power. Pharrell and Chad learned to play guitars soon afterwards. Pharrell has explained all this flux by simply saying that The Neptunes and N*E*R*D are two different entities, and thus should sound different. If the aim was to make music that showed they weren't "just" producers, that much had been achieved.

Named after the Leonard Nimoy-hosted TV show, *In Search Of*... is a major success, perhaps oddly, given its complicated twin-conception. On their website they described the band thus: "N*E*R*D is the offspring of The Neptunes' id, a fly-or-die, thrash-around, do-as-you-will, set-your-soul-on-fire alter ego that subscribes to no rules, and adheres to no agenda. It is Pharrell, Chad and Shay – a trio whose chemistry allows the uninhibited exploration of the sounds, emotions and impulses of self and society, of identity and belonging. Of life."

Pharrell, as N*E*R*D's lead singer, has also, in a characteristically gnomic or wayward stab at clarification, discussed the philosophy and beliefs behind that peculiar band name. "N*E*R*D stands for No One Ever Really Dies. The Neptunes are who we are and N*E*R*D is what we do. It's our life. N*E*R*D is just a basic belief, man. People's energies are made of their souls. When you die, that energy may disperse, but it isn't destroyed. Energy cannot be destroyed. It can manifest in a different way, but even then it's like their souls are going somewhere. If it's going to heaven and hell or even if it's going into a fog or somewhere in the atmosphere to lurk unbeknownst to itself, it's going somewhere."

As is common throughout pop history whenever a name act switches course and delivers a curveball, the press were confused and divided. Most reviews were positive, as is demonstrated by some of the following lines of enthusiasm. *Rolling Stone* said, "The music is good – it's a crunch groove that's part Timbaland, part Afrika Bambaataa and part *Star Trek* on ecstasy." *Spin* wrote of the reframed rock version: "Ace genre-mashing... the addition of a band makes the record weirder, punching up the rock that was merely implicit on the previous version. That's 'rock' as in rap-rock, alt-rock and Paisley Park psych-rock." *Q* magazine (naming it among their best fifty albums of 2001) thought it "a striking escape from mere genre. A swaggering, rock-friendly counterpart to the likes of Outkast. And no less essential either." *Uncut* also compared it to Outkast's *Stankonia* album, while for RapReviews.com it was "a musical experiment – a joyride for The Neptunes to go crazy on. And it works." *NME* liked its "fuzzy-warm highs, hazy cosmic visions and exquisite ripples in the fabric of R&B as we know it", while *Mojo* name-checked Jimi Hendrix, Sly Stone, Eminem and Funkadelic. *Alternative Press* saw a similarity to "modern metal".

However, esteemed US critic Robert Christgau was more sceptical. While acknowledging that it (the first version of the album) was "annoyingly catchy", he suggested "they call themselves N*E*R*D because that's what they are – nerds at their worst. Sure, they're clever, but they're also as shallow as Britney Spears, who I swear they're dumb enough to want to f***." Yet when the rock version emerged, he revised his viewpoint. "I now love it for the same reasons I panned it. Obscenely wealthy, obscenely catchy thugs-by-association rationalize their ethics and throw their dicks around, only they're consumed by doubt and hence honest enough to make themselves look like jerks."

Whatever they made of Mr Christgau's fiery opinion, N*E*R*D were not unhappy to be provocative. Pharrell Williams had always spoken of his admiration for Eminem. "He was our middle finger to the corporates," he said. "Those corporate guys didn't really care for us (black hip-hop acts) too much, but Eminem was like their own son letting you know that he loves hip-hop. Now you have to recant everything you ever said, because hip-hop is your children, and suburban America. It's gotten to where you've got Republicans saying they liked (the film) *8 Mile*. They're now hearing us. Eminem, thank you sir. You've made them hate you, and now they love you, and I love it. You're doing a great service to hip-hop right now."

Speaking to VH1, he further eulogised the best-selling act in America of the 2000s and his influence on the musical landscape. "Now hip-hop has become big business. People use the same marketing strategies that they use on toilet tissues and candy bars for marketing videos and songs. Those corporate dudes realized how much money was in it. Did you ever think you'd see the day when hip-hop actually sold more than Barbra Streisand? Even when stars like Streisand put their greatest hits out, they might get number one for the first week, but Eminem's gonna come and slaughter you the next week."

These days, Pharrell is no stranger to corporate marketing strategies himself, but at this point he was still willing - at least for a while - to play the angry young provocateur. The lead single from N*E*R*D was 'Lapdance' (featuring Lee Harvey and Vita), and its video, set in a strip club, drew much opprobrium from those who deemed it sexist and degrading to women. "I'm a dirty dog," muttered Pharrell over the opening, and the words got filthier from there. *Rolling Stone* deadpanned: "If you're a fan of watching dudes' faces when multiple girls are grinding on them, you've found your new favourite video." A weirdly moustachioed Pharrell and his cohorts were seen "grinding" with topless, near-naked females (in the uncensored version), and it's safe to say the video didn't win any feminist points. (Kelis can be spotted in the video too, as a casual observer). This was a long, long way away from the children happy-clapping of 2013's 'Happy', but perhaps came from the similar part of his psyche as the equally controversial collaboration with Robin Thicke, 'Blurred Lines', which also upset many.

Years later, discussing 'Blurred Lines', Pharrell attempted to defend these unpleasantly chauvinist attitudes. "Is it sexist when you walk around in a museum and a lot of the statues have their boobs out?" he asked. "The women in the video were only dancing. I didn't do anything sexually suggestive to any of those women, I wouldn't allow it. I have respect and I know the message that I want to put out. I'm a fun guy. I love women. I know their importance."

Nonetheless the controversy of course grabbed attention, and 'Lapdance' made it into the top twenty in the UK and the Hot R&B chart in the US. Trent Reznor of Nine Inch Nails later remixed it, and it has popped up in films such as *Daredevil* and *Kiss Of The Dragon*.

'Rock Star' and 'Provider' followed as the next N*E*R*D singles. The former (which wasn't averse to swearing) was given a profile boost by featuring in an iPod TV advert, and got to number 15 in the UK. It was also the outfit's first single to chart in Australia. A video by Hype Williams was shot but then mysteriously shelved. 'Provider' came out as a double A-side with a re-release of 'Lapdance'. Its video showed Pharrell and Chad riding around with a bike gang, and starred actors Brad Renfro and Kelli Garner. Pusha T of Clipse appeared as a drug dealer.

While *In Search Of...* did contain songs about loving someone for her "brain", and proved that The Neptunes team weren't one-trick ponies, it's often a grubby, unsavoury affair, with salacious tales of taping sexual acts and young groupies. There are some long-time hardcore fans that feel Pharrell Williams has "sold out" since then. Others might argue that he's simply grown up. Chad Hugo once said, "Pharrell is more quirky in real life than he is in videos and on other people's songs." Shay Haley added, "He is a little more eccentric in his personality, and in N*E*R*D he can pull that off."

When N*E*R*D played live, Pharrell came across as relatively relaxed and unflashy onstage. As the *Chicago Tribune* recorded in 2002 when they played that city's Metro venue, Williams and Hugo had "thoroughly dominated pop and R&B radio in the last few years with often surprisingly unconventional songwriting, arranging and beat-shaping for Britney Spears, Jay-Z, Mystikal and countless others." There was, it added, "an off-handed dirtiness to these productions that appeals to both pop programmers and hip-hop connoisseurs, with staccato sandpaper beats fattened by digital production. Now, the Neptunes are trying to bring the same loose-limbed charm to their performing incarnation, known as N*E*R*D." Hugo wasn't even there, but Spymob backed the combo. "The Neptunes/ N*E*R*D aren't easily pinned down, the cheeseball sides of their personalities dancing with genius, irony trafficking with sincerity, outsider subversion walking with we-are-the-world idealism." Spymob came across as a "blue-eyed soul-pop band...versatile and workmanlike", and Williams and Haley lacked "the swagger of hip-hop's giants. It is exactly this ordinariness that is N*E*R*D's niche in a crowded field; they're the voice of the audience that falls between the cracks of hip-hop's macho boasting and pop's smarmy romanticism."

The review went on to note Williams's "regular-guy persona" and "guileless tone", suggesting he sang with unselfconscious verve "whether he's praising a potential lover for her 'Brain' or pleading to document a lesbian encounter in 'Tape You'. "We're about breaking rules," Pharrell announced. Kelis made a guest appearance in a show that saw a "bi-racial band saluting its multiracial audience, a nation of open-minded outsiders bonding over misfit music that has improbably taken over the charts."

Kelis must not be overlooked in this chapter of The Neptunes' evolution. Her debut album had been crucial to their learning curve, and the follow-up, *Wanderland*, released in 2001, was another full Neptunes production. Perhaps less poppy and more experimental than *Kaleidoscope*, it failed to match the commercial success of that minor classic. In fact Virgin Records didn't release it in the States, fearing it lacked singles. In Europe, 'Young Fresh 'n' New' proved a minor hit, and the album sold moderately at best. (She was to bounce back with 2003's *Tasty*, and The Neptunes' gem 'Milkshake'.) A version of the track 'Popular Thug', replacing Pusha T of Clipse with Nas, emerged again on *The Neptunes Present... Clones* two years later. *The Guardian* hailed *Wanderland* as "clever, exhilarating and original", while *Entertainment Weekly* praised "a more coherent artistry than many recent boundary-busting experiments". However, *Slant* magazine thought that "The Neptunes' rehashed retro beats and synths are beginning to sound derivative... unchallenging and repetitive".

A couple more link-ups in Pharrell's peripatetic year of 2001 should be mentioned. No Doubt guested on the Kelis album, and the Pharrell connection/friendship with Gwen Stefani – he also worked on No Doubt's 'Hella Good' – was of course to bear fruit subsequently. And The Neptunes remixed 'Harder, Better, Faster, Stronger' from the Daft

Punk album of that year, sending them into the top three of the US Hot Dance chart...

Next though, it was time to get *Justified*.

CHAPTER 5
PRODUCING THE FUTURE

Among the lengthy credits of Justin Timberlake's quadruple-platinum album *Justified*, you can find Justin writing: "Special thanks to all the producers who helped me create my own sound. Pharrell – you were essential in making the album. Thanks for being my friend. The world is ours. A special shout-out to Chad 'Hip-Hop' Hugo, my favourite Filipino. Timbaland – you helped me take some chances on this album that I know I couldn't have done with anyone else. I can't wait 'til the next one." Neither could several million fans, as *Justified* rocketed Timberlake from generic boy band star and Britney Spears' ex-beau to Grammy-winning global pop icon. Another triumph for Williams and Hugo was acknowledged, as *Slant* magazine opined that he meshed with The Neptunes "so well he virtually relinquishes his personality to the super-duo. He could very well be the third member of N*E*R*D." This was perhaps a little harsh: Timberlake exuded pop-star sex appeal and easy charisma, comfortably moving on from his teen-pop background, but it reiterated the influence and impact of The Neptunes on the contemporary music scene.

The signs were auspicious from the off. "We (Chad and Pharrell) picked him up right after he checked in at his hotel in Virginia Beach," Chad Hugo told MTV. "We drove around in the car listening to old Earth, Wind & Fire albums, and he was totally with it. The background of those songs is the feeling we wanted to incorporate into the music. He was like, 'Nobody's ever heard anything like that before... a white boy singing this kind of music...' He didn't care what people would say."

And when Justin enjoyed phenomenal success with the star-making songs, it emerged that they could have been snapped up by no less a figure than "The King Of Pop" Michael Jackson. The Neptunes had offered a bundle to Jackson's management, who had taken the decision to pass on them. "Some of the songs were offered to Michael Jackson first, yes," confirmed Pharrell. "But his manager said they weren't good enough so they were given to Justin instead." It will remain high in the history of what-ifs to ponder what Jacko would have done with the distinctly *Off The Wall*-influenced 'Rock Your Body' or 'Let's Take A Ride'. (Usher's 'U Don't Have To Call' is also said to have been written with Jackson in mind). Some instrumental tracks from the demos were used within *Justified*. "It would have been great with Michael but Justin is my boy," clarified Pharrell. "I'm so glad it turned out the way it did, because that was a wonderful experience for us to do that kind of work and for those songs to be brought to life."

With the key influences of Jackson and Earth, Wind & Fire, the Neptunes-Timberlake team-up was a dream of light funk. "I was raised on Earth, Wind & Fire," said Pharrell. "'Can't Hide Love' from the album *Gratitude* was the first record that influenced my life. My mom and dad used to play this song a lot when I was a kid. It changed me. I think it's what made me a singer. In fact Earth, Wind & Fire are probably what made *me*, full stop – that's baby-making music, man!"

Pharrell also later recalled a meeting with Michael Jackson, and what a fan he'd been of the legendary performer. "I remember watching them (The Jacksons) on television when I was really young, when the record 'Shake Your Body (Down To The Ground)' came out, around 1978. Did it influence my vocal style? I can't sing like him. I think my vocal style is just what I could scram together. The *Thriller* album also changed my life. So did 'Billie Jean'."

"The songs I wrote for Justin Timberlake's album *Justified*, I originally wrote for Michael, although we modified them a bit. I told Michael that, and he was like, 'You're kidding me! You're kidding me! That's so wonderful!' Then he sang them in Justin's style. He could sing just like Justin, or R. Kelly... he was one of the most incredible performers of all time. And he was also by far one of the best beat-boxers ever..."

In another interview, with Nitsuh Abebe, Pharrell recalled his encounter with Michael, and the fate of the songs, slightly differently. "All those songs – with the exception of 'Like I Love You' – were songs I made for Michael Jackson. His manager didn't like them. Somehow I think Michael didn't like them either, though. Because when I finally met him, he sang all those songs back to me, and said, 'Those songs should have been for me.' And he just laughed... But he sang those songs to me and sang them just like Justin. Then he sang 'U Don't Have To Call' (the Neptunes-penned Usher hit), the way I'd written it. They were for him. He sang those songs to me, so he kinda knew... but at the same time they just weren't good enough."

They were certainly good enough for most people, and the 21-year-old Timberlake was sharp enough to know it. The album has sold more than eight million copies. Upon its release on 5 November 2002, the promotional campaign led with: "Here it is – one of the most talked-about and eagerly awaited albums of the year. There are few artists who truly deserve the title of superstar – Justin Timberlake is undoubtedly one of them. As one fifth of the multiplatinum *NYSNC, he's responsible for the monster hits 'Pop', 'Gone' and 'Girlfriend', and combined album sales of over thirty million worldwide. As co-writer on all his debut album's thirteen tracks, Justin proves his songwriting talents again. The first cut, 'Like I Love You', was the perfect introduction to *Justified*. It became a huge hit and mirrored the success of (The Neptunes' co-write with Justin) 'Girlfriend' by merging urban and pop fans into one unit. The Neptunes also feature on the album, as do Timbaland, Bubba Sparxx, Clipse, Scott Storch, Janet Jackson and Brian McKnight..."

Indeed, 'Like I Love You' (featuring a rap verse by long-time Neptunes' allies Clipse) had proven the perfect launch single for Timberlake's solo career. A US Billboard Hot 100 chart number 11 and a UK number two, it was showcased by J.T. at the MTV Video Music Awards in New York City on 29 August. (It picked up a Grammy nomination the next year for Best Rap/Sung collaboration). Pharrell reiterated that the rhythms were a homage to the funk era. Chad Hugo added that, "We just wanted to recreate that sense of those timeless, classic songs, without any of the 'bling-bling, hit me on my two-way' style of the new R&B. It has elements of the old and the new." The first song written and recorded by the trio, with Hugo and Williams playing everything, it again asserted that The Neptunes had the Midas touch. Said Timberlake, "It sounded so original to me. And I kind of consider myself a new artist. This is a new beginning for me, so why call on some big-name hip-hop artist when I could get somebody that feels new... it feels like we're both chomping at the bit at the same time."

Critics concurred with the fans. "Over a lo-fi Neptunes-produced track dashed with Spanish guitar, live drums and Planet Rock-like electro bleeps," offered *Entertainment Weekly's* Craig Seymour, "Justin proves that while no innovator, he is a fine student." "Minimalism influenced by Michael Jackson... pleasing teen girls and beat junkies alike," wrote *Rolling Stone*. BBC Music thought it "one of the best Neptunes productions this year".

Pharrell made a brief "Hitchcockian" cameo in the 'Like I Love You' video, although Hitchcock wasn't much of a one for body-popping. Williams didn't think anyone would notice. "Only you caught that!" he told *The Guardian's* eagle-eyed interviewer Paul Lester in 2004. "It was like: woah, we did something there! That's what it was. You're the only person in the world who caught that. I just remember thinking: we're gonna f*** 'em up with this."

Written and recorded in six weeks, *Justified* was described by Timberlake as a "creative spurt...(like) that period back in the 1960s and 70s when musicians got together and just jammed and worked out of inspiration. There was no heavy calculation or belabouring songs and mixes. Everything flowed pretty easily and naturally." The Neptunes collaborated on no less than seven of the tracks, and after 'Cry Me A River' became the second hit (boosted by rumours it was Justin baring his soul about his break-up with Britney), their classic *Off The Wall/Thriller* homage 'Rock Your Body' became the third. Released on 6 May 2003, it rose into the top five in almost every country, winning certifications of gold in the US and platinum in Australia. 'Senorita', another Neptunes jam, "*featuring* Pharrell", kept up the run of hits.

As late as February 2004, 'Rock Your Body' soundtracked one of the memorable pop-cultural moments of the year, when Timberlake performed the song with Janet Jackson in front of vast audiences at the Super Bowl XXXVIII half-time show. As he sang the line, "Bet I'll have you naked by the end of this song", he tore off part of Jackson's costume, "accidentally" (they both swear) exposing her right breast on live TV. The phrase "wardrobe malfunction" was born. After a storm of criticism, Timberlake suggested that "America is harsher on women, and unfairly harsh on ethnic people."

Justified couldn't stop selling, however, and some commentators remarked that Michael Jackson had missed a trick in not taking Pharrell and Chad's songs: "the ultra-modern R&B-pop hybrid." Timberlake won the American Music Award for Favourite Pop/Rock Album, and two Grammys the following year. The album stayed on the charts in the States for seventy-two weeks, though quirkily it never made number one (thwarted in its first fortnight by Eminem's *8 Mile* soundtrack). In the UK, it was number one for seven (non-consecutive) weeks, going five times platinum.

As if all this wasn't enough to keep Justin, Pharrell and Chad in expensive hats, their jingle for a well-known burger conglomerate was next to prove a nice little earner. 'I'm Lovin' It' – written by Pharrell, Tom Batoy, Andreas Forberger and Franco Tortora, produced by The Neptunes – was a song released by Timberlake in November 2003, which featured in McDonalds adverts. Timberlake was announced as McDonalds' new "spokesman", and the company sponsored his world tour (which commenced soon after his North American tour with Christina Aguilera). "I love what McDonalds is doing with the 'I'm Lovin' It' campaign," said Justin, "and it's cool to be a part of it. We share the same crowd – people who like to have fun."

Pharrell Williams had come a mighty long way since his days of being repeatedly fired by the McDonalds bosses. Presumably he now felt justified. The year 2002 had also seen The Neptunes land a Nike commercial, but they were far from done with bossing the charts. From here on, it gets too hectic to list every single track they dipped in gold dust, but as well as work with Solange, Toni Braxton, LL Cool J and Sean Paul, they enjoyed monster hits with Nelly's 'Hot In Herre' and Snoop Dogg's 'Beautiful'. The former, boasting typically suggestive lyrics ("so take off all your clothes"), was one of that summer's ubiquitous dance-floor favourites. Using a hook from Chuck Brown and The Soul Searchers' 'Bustin' Loose' of 1978, and sampling everyone from Nancy Sinatra to Neil Young, it was an enormous and effervescent Billboard number one. The smouldering album *Nellyville* (on which Timberlake guested), also a chart-topper, became one of the best-selling rap albums of all time.

"I knew 'Hot In Herre' was gonna be a great song, but I didn't know it was going to be as massive as it was," admitted Pharrell to *Vulture* magazine. "Because I love that feeling, that Chuck Brown go-go feeling, I knew it was gonna go, but I didn't know it was gonna go to a number one record. Whenever I thought something was going to be huge, it always superseded what I meant by 'huge'. 'Huge' was like, 'it's gonna be a big record, a top ten record, and people will love it'. I didn't know (it would be)... record-breaking! I've always been humbled by that kind of stuff."

The "humbling" year closed out with the release of iconic rapper Snoop Dogg's sixth album, *Paid Tha Cost To Be Da Boss*. This platinum, million-seller included two prime Neptunes cuts, which led the release as its (only) two singles. "The most spirited pop record of his career," raved *Spin*. "Snoop stretches his silky flow," wrote *Rolling Stone*, "over tracks by underground ace Hi-Tek and the unstoppable Neptunes."

First single 'From Tha Chuuuch To Da Palace' contained re-sung elements from The Isley Brothers' 'Contagious'. Pharrell was getting his face in the videos again, except this time he was disguised as, believe it or not, Bill Gates. More conventional, and with an enviable Rio de Janeiro beach/carnival setting that wowed viewers worldwide, was the 'Beautiful' video, which helped that single go platinum. Pharrell was front and centre, buddying up with Snoop (and, of course, copious gorgeous models, despite the song reportedly being written about Snoop's daughter).

Again, Pharrell expressed surprise at the sweep of its success. "I like to say that 65 per cent of the time I know when it's going to kill," he told *Vulture* magazine. "Or I'll have that feeling. That doesn't mean I'm always 65 per cent right. The other 35 per cent I'm really surprised."

After another giddy year of runaway hits and stellar collaborations, with Chad Hugo seemingly content to take a backroom role away from the limelight, Pharrell was in the unusual position of being all over the charts, magazines and screens of the world, without having his own record out. Catching and blowing. It was time to start frontin'.

CHAPTER 6
THE MIDAS MAN

2003 was the golden year in which statistics claimed that The Neptunes (and more specifically, Pharrell, including all his guest appearances) were responsible – as producers or performers – for a staggering 43 per cent of all music played on USA radio and 20 per cent of all music played on UK radio. That's quite phenomenal. Surely nobody has enjoyed domination like

that – though of course the man himself was to effectively match it for impact a decade on with his 'Get Lucky'/'Blurred Lines'/'Happy' triple-threat. Reminded of the spectacular numbers by *The Guardian's* Paul Lester in 2004, he was characteristically cryptic, saying, "Thank you, that's quite a compliment... (but) we just want to make good music. Credit isn't to be taken, it's to be given."

Understandably, or bravely, Pharrell felt the urge to venture out on his own, to put his own face to a hit record. His solo music career began with a dipping-of-toes-into-the-water on the debut single 'Frontin''. He wrote and sang it; The Neptunes produced. A summer hit, released in June, it featured appropriately A-list guest Jay-Z rapping and ended up ranked as one of the biggest Stateside hits of the year. Back then, Pharrell insisted it was a one-off gambit, and that he was a producer not a solo artist. Events persuaded him otherwise, though it was another three years before his first solo album, and even longer after that before his second.

'Frontin'' was, on the surface, a jibe at putting up false facades to impress friends, but the video nonetheless portrayed Pharrell taking his shirt off to show off his torso, as ladies (Lanisha Cole and Lauren London) swooned. The track peaked in the top five on the Billboard Hot 100 and the top six in the UK. British pop-jazz singer Jamie Cullum covered it, also having a hit, and Pharrell was so keen on this version that he asked Cullum to provide some backing vocals on his 2006 solo album. Some, including rapper Mos Def, noticed similarities in feel between 'Frontin'' and A Tribe Called Quest's 1990 hit 'Bonita Applebum'. Pharrell openly admitted he had always loved that track, almost to the point of youthful obsession.

"'Bonita Applebum' was the first single from the album *People's Instinctive Travels And The Paths Of Rhythm*," Pharrell recalled. "And my friend in Virginia got hold of a copy of it. I was so amazed by that record that I lost my mind. I didn't know what it was, I was like, 'Oh my god!' I played it day in, day out. Every girl I dated had to listen to it over and over late at night, and we had to have nightly discussions about it. We needed to talk about how it took us to other worlds. Those girls are all probably laughing right now, thinking: 'Damn, he was a musician, but didn't know it! That's why we had to do all that dumb shit and talk about it all night!' Because I'd be, like, 'You have to listen to this! If you don't listen to this we're finished!' After 'Bonita Applebum', I went to the other side, and started making music rather than just listening."

A Pharrell album didn't follow immediately, but the first album under The Neptunes' brand name did, in August. *The Neptunes Present...Clones* was a "various artists" record, produced by Pharrell and "power behind the throne" Chad. It gathered collaborations with friends old and new. 'Frontin'' was the first single, and three more hotly pursued it: 'Light Your Ass On Fire' by Busta Rhymes featuring

Pharrell, 'Hot Damn' by Clipse and 'It Blows My Mind' by Snoop Dogg. Demonstrating that the public were already very aware of The Neptunes, it raced straight to number one in the US, soon going gold, with opening-week sales of more than 250,000. Among other parties appearing on the album were Kelis, Nas, Ludacris, Nelly, Spymob, Vanessa Marquez, Dirt McGirt, Pusha-T, N.O.R.E. and Jadakiss.

It also served as notice that the Star Trak label was a highly viable entity. Amid their hectic opening years of the century, Pharrell and Chad had founded their own label in 2001. Partially funded by Arista, it allowed The Neptunes to sign long-time friends Clipse (brothers Pusha-T and No Malice), whose album *Lord Willin'* they'd released in 2002. They then signed Kelis (whose hit album *Tasty* emerged on the label), Fam-Lay, Vanessa Marquez, Spymob and their own alter egos N*E*R*D. In 2004 the label's imprint moved from Arista to EMI's Virgin, and put out the second N*E*R*D album. Albums by Snoop Dogg, Robin Thicke and Pharrell himself were to follow, in time.

The Neptunes' album was moderately well-received by reviewers. Said *Rolling Stone's* Kelefa Sanneh, "Williams and Hugo have made themselves indispensable (to any rapper in need of a hit)... so now it's time to show off." Describing the record as a sampler for their label, the review added that, "with wall-to-wall Neptunes beats, this should be the world's greatest hip-hop compilation, and much of the time it is." But while praising Ludacris in particular, it sniffed at Pharrell and Chad's own cuts. "They should be better. 'Loser', by their alter ego

N*E*R*D, welds a great, breezy riff to a lame chorus. Pharrell's slow-jam, 'Frontin'', sounds more like an extended joke than a song, despite the Jay-Z verse. The Neptunes may be the greatest pushers around, but that doesn't mean they can do without their clients." *Rap Reviews* summed up pragmatically: "This much is sure – you won't have to guess who produced any of the tracks on this album."

Importantly, Pharrell had stepped out from behind the wizard's curtain, and earned his performing spurs. Meanwhile, the production and guest-spot work continued apace, featuring ever-bigger and more diverse names. In 2003, they worked on Beyoncé's 'My First Time' (which ultimately failed to make the cut for her superstar breakthrough *Dangerously In Love* album), and with her paramour Jay-Z (Pharrell appearing in the 'Change Clothes' video), and remixed Jennifer Lopez's 'Love Don't Cost A Thing'. Pharrell guested with Foxy Brown and with Nas, and The Neptunes released Kelis's third album *Tasty*. N*E*R*D guested with Papa Roach, and The Neptunes even remixed rock giants The Rolling Stones's 'Sympathy For The Devil'.

Kelis, in many ways, had got the ball rolling for the pair, and *Tasty* bounced back strongly from the relative flop of *Wanderland*, promoting her to star status. The Neptunes handled five of its fourteen cuts (Dallas Austin and Andre 3000 also got involved), and were responsible for the major Grammy-nominated hit 'Milkshake'. ('Trick Me', 'Millionaire' and 'In Public' were also hits, giving Star Trak a very successful album on both sides of the Atlantic). Kelis was "a parallel universe Beyoncé", thought *The Guardian*, "exploiting her husky croon like never before, pouring it over lascivious double entendre". The ebullient euphemism of 'Milkshake', as it brought all the boys to the yard, was defined by Kelis as "that something which makes women special". She later went as far as to say that the track's sexual confidence was a watershed for music, suggesting, "It literally changed female vocalists".

Pharrell claimed he still didn't realize quite what a celebrity he'd become. "The funny thing is, I don't feel like a star," he protested to *The Guardian's* Paul Lester, even as the paparazzi gathered outside the London hotel where the interview was taking place. "Being in newspapers, being rumoured to be messing with this girl or messing with that girl – that's not what I got into this business for."

"I don't consider myself a pin-up," he continued. "I'm not one of those dudes in magazines with insane muscles. If I was, I wish it would do me some good and get me a girlfriend." Wrote Lester, "This is curious coming from one of the most eligible bachelors alive, although not as curious as his next pronouncement: 'I'd like to apologise to my future wife, but I've been busy doing an album for the people.'" (Indeed, although workaholic Pharrell was to become a father in 2008, he and the mother didn't marry until 2013.)

The album Pharrell was now "busy" with "for the people" was a second N*E*R*D offering, *Fly Or Die*. The "alter egos" of The Neptunes played their "real" instruments this time, so that they could perform the tracks live without the full-time assistance of Spymob. The album, just over an hour long, was recorded throughout 2003 in Virginia Beach and Los Angeles and came out on 23 March 2004, selling half a million copies as it leaped into the top ten, winning RIAA gold certification. Guest performers included members of rock outfit Good Charlotte on 'Jump', while Lenny Kravitz and Questlove of The Roots appeared on 'Maybe'.

Speaking to the VH1 channel, Pharrell explained elements of the philosophy behind the album and its title. "*Fly or Die* is the only choice an eagle's egg hatching in mid air that fell out of its mother's nest would have. The only choice you have in life is to fly or die. I felt the title for so many reasons. That's where the world was (when we named it). We're either going to fly together or die together. For me, in my relentless pursuit of love, it's either fly or die: be optimistic or wither away into nothing. That should be everybody's motto in life. Go for it. If you don't go for it, you're going to lose it."

And the more publicly reticent Chad Hugo had a few words to say on the album too, on the band's website. "It's evolution. For real. There's an entire dimension to music and life that we touched on with *In Search Of...*, but that was only the beginning. Those were only doors to this other dimension, and with this album we are there... I think we learned a lot from the first album, and we've opened up more here. I think we're going places we haven't gone before." As to the challenge of playing live, Chad clarified, "We've always played our own instruments in everything we do, but we convert them into programming for the final tracks. For *Fly Or Die*, we decided to pick up the instruments and play ourselves and leave it like that. It's more honest, and people don't know this side of us yet."

'She Wants To Move', the lead single (featuring 4Motel), was an international hit. Its video became an MTV favourite, and featured well-known British singer (now television personality and *Britain's Got Talent* judge) Alesha Dixon, once of garage-pop girl band and 'Scandalous' hit-makers Mis-Teeq. Other more would-be profound tracks dealt with typically adolescent-teenage problems, such as bullying (on 'Thrasher'), conscription and rebellious tendencies (on 'Drill Sergeant'), and horniness (on 'Backseat Love', though Pharrell had "addressed" this "issue" many times before and has continued to since).

As Neptunes-love was now not just fashionable but mandatory, reviews were glowing. "This is an enthusiastic hymn to the terminally uncool," wrote *Mojo*, "(and) an un-ironic celebration of nerd culture. They make a party you want to be invited to." "It's fascinating," said *Rolling Stone*, "to hear these rap geniuses go undercover as a bar band you might hear rocking Journey covers in a bowling alley." Less encouragingly, the magazine then went on to compare the sound to Sammy Hagar's solo career. *Entertainment Weekly* considered *Fly Or Die* "craftier and more multi-layered than its predecessor. A set of clever, complex, studio-crafted pop, complete with smooth-jazz licks, that doesn't owe allegiance to any one genre." *Uncut* magazine, bizarrely, thought the album to be "eclectic art-rock" and "prog-pop album of the year", comparing it to 10CC and XTC. *The Guardian's* Alexis Petridis was less enthused, concluding that "*Fly Or Die* falls flat", but did confirm the album's bewildering range by citing references to The Beatles, The Lovin' Spoonful, Queens Of The Stone Age and Genesis. *The New York Times* chipped in that, "While Mr Williams isn't much of a singer, *Fly Or Die* has goofy charms to spare."

Mr Williams pressed on with flying. Asked by Paul Lester what girl-fans said to him when they hugged him, he shrugged, "You know, the 'I love you' stuff. 'I love your music, I love you, marry me'. All those flattering things. Shit, I still ain't got over getting a Grammy for The Neptunes as Producers Of The Year. I'm afraid of getting over those things. To say, 'Yeah, I'm a Grammy award-winning guy', I'm afraid to say that. I just think everything will come tumbling down after that." Did his fame prevent him from doing things he really wanted to do? "It's cool," he replied. "I have no complaints, man. Tired, but no complaints. I could be somewhere else, doing something I really don't want to do."

Fortune favours the bold, and for the fortunate Pharrell, everything was not about to come tumbling down.

With his hit song 'Happy' Pharrell won Grammys for both Best Music Video and Best Pop Solo Performance in 2015 – and he accepted the awards in shorts.

Since meeting as children, Pharrell, Shay Haley (*centre*) and Chad Hugo (*right*) have released four albums and enjoyed enormous success as N*E*R*D.

Pharrell has collaborated with Justin Timberlake a number of times over his career. He is just one of the big names to have benefited from Pharrell's creative expertise.

An early shot of Pharrell from the Princess Anne High School yearbook.

Performing with Jay-Z on *MTV Unplugged* in 2001.

Getting inked by Mister Cartoon in Los Angeles.

In March 2014 Pharrell was announced as a new coach on the popular TV talent show *The Voice*.

Pictured with Al Gore and Cameron Diaz at a 'Save our Selves' press conference, Pharrell has been an activist for a number of important political causes over the years.

One incredible birthday cake was unveiled by Pharrell at his Spongebob-themed 41st birthday party.

One of the biggest hits of the twenty-first century was Pharrell's controversial 'Blurred Lines' which he wrote and performed with Robin Thicke.

Possibly the most unconventional of his collaborators, the innovative Daft Punk enjoyed a great deal of success with Pharrell.

'Happy' wasn't just a hit song but a global phenomenon of immense cultural and political significance – which is some achievement for a song from an animated children's film.

CHAPTER 7
FLY OR DIE

"This s*** is bananas. B.A.N.A.N.A.S.!" So rang out the catchy breakdown refrain from Gwen Stefani's 'Hollaback Girl', one of 2005's most popular songs. A number one in the USA and Australia, it became the first digital download to sell a million in the United States. It was, needless to say, another Neptunes production and co-write, as Pharrell forged a friendship with Stefani that

stayed strong a decade on: in 2014 the pair – both coaches on the American version of *The Voice* – were recording together again.

Stefani's 2004 album *Love. Angel. Music. Baby.* had seen her branch out from being the vocalist with pop-rock-ska outfit No Doubt to shine as a solo star. With collaborators like Dr Dre, Andre 3000, Linda Perry and Dallas Austin (as well as The Neptunes) it was always going to be a hit, but few predicted it would go multi-platinum, selling over seven million worldwide. Influenced by Eighties pop, bearing themes of fashion and wealth, it was fun, bling, and credible. Offering singles like 'What You Waiting For?', 'Rich Girl', 'Luxurious' and 'Cool', it was called by *Yahoo! Music* "the hottest, coolest, best-dressed pop album of the year". BBC Music hailed it as "a stunning and stylish effort that showcases Gwen's credentials as a bona fide pop goddess." "Frivolously brilliant," said *NME*.

Yet it was 'Hollaback Girl' that best captured the album's crackle, colour and identity. After grunge singer Courtney Love had dismissed Stefani as a "cheerleader", Gwen said, "And I've never been a cheerleader. So I was like: OK, you want me to be a cheerleader? Well I'll be one then, and I'll rule the whole world. Just watch me." She told Pharrell she wanted an "attitude" song, but also "a silly dance record". With shades of Toni Basil's Eighties hit 'Mickey', 'Hollaback Girl' was infectiously buoyant.

The Neptunes had written with Stefani earlier in the process, but she has said she lacked confidence then and fell prey to writer's block. With the album nearly completed, her confidence returning, she flew to New York to resume work with Pharrell. Here, he played her his forthcoming solo album, of which she felt "envious"... but she was also inspired. On the resulting 'Hollaback Girl', she said, "To me, it is the freshest attitude song I've heard in so long." Said Pharrell, "Gwen is like the girl in high school who just had her own style." "A trademark Neptunes hip-hop stomp," wrote Playlouder, while *Rolling Stone* reckoned that "Gwen's gum-snapping sass brings out the beast in her beatmasters." On the 2005 end-of-year chart, the single was number two, beaten only by Mariah Carey's 'We Belong Together'.

The bananas Pharrell-Gwen hip-hop hook-up was to yield further fruit, with Stefani ultimately guesting on the lead track and first single from Williams's overdue, much-delayed debut solo album *In My Mind*. This though was pushed back more than once from its initial planned release date, with Pharrell's "perfectionist" tendencies being given as the reason. Still, he had plenty of distractions. In 2004 there were further tracks with Nelly ('Flap Your Wings'), Cee-Lo Green ('Let's Stay Together', 'The Art Of Noise') and Snoop Dogg. The Snoop album *Rhythm & Gangsta (The Masterpiece)* yielded the instant classics 'Drop It Like It's Hot' and 'Let's Get Blown', as well as 'Signs', 'Pass It Pass' and 'Perfect'.

Taken from the platinum, million-selling album *Sweat*, the effervescent 'Flap Your Wings' was a Nelly-Chad-Pharrell co-write produced by The Neptunes. Cee-Lo's second album *...Is The Soul Machine* benefited from two Neptunes tracks, though it wasn't until 2006's Gnarls Barkley smash 'Crazy' that the big man broke big. The Snoop album – which has now sold more than three million – followed up the Neptunes link on 'Beautiful' with an even more outstanding single. 'Drop It Like It's Hot', featuring Pharrell on the first verse (into which he dropped a line from 'Raspy Shit', which would feature on his solo debut), was noted for its sparse, minimalist tongue-clicking structure. It became Snoop's first number one on the Billboard Hot 100. Its successors 'Let's Get Blown' and then 'Signs' (featuring Justin Timberlake) further confirmed the Neptunes' international chart domination. This despite a *Pitchfork* review that erroneously declared that they were on the wane. Of *Rhythm & Gangsta*, Tom Breihan wrote, "Snoop's first album for Star Trak, the label run by fallen-off hip-hop hitmakers The Neptunes, a duo who all but ruled international radio with dazzling sci-fi stomp-clap new wave beats, but who've been starving for hits ever since they switched their style to overcooked Vegas schmaltz – all bloopy bass and shuffling drums and swooshing keyboards and unbelievably obnoxious falsetto crooning..." Such rumours of Pharrell's demise were, needless to say, greatly exaggerated. 'Drop It Like It's Hot' was Pharrell's biggest ever worldwide hit as a performer, up to that point. In 2009, Billboard named it "Rap Song of the Decade".

While that solo album was cooking in the kitchen, some wondered if Chad Hugo was concerned at the possibilities of a Neptunes split. Far from it. In fact, Pharrell sang his praises on the record. The Neptunes remained a thriving and productive parallel outfit. Said a supportive Chad, who took on extracurricular solo production work himself, "We came from a small town, which makes you kinda go through a lot. Virginia is sorta like this nine-to-five town, and our parents probably didn't even expect us to take our music this far. We started out at band camp, and we thought that was going to be it after a while. But we took that love, and applied it, and I think his message is that you could do it too. And that's how I feel when I listen to his stuff."

At last Pharrell's solo album saw the light of day. In September 2005 the single 'Can I Have It Like That' led the way. It featured Gwen Stefani, who had heard the material while the pair were working on her song 'Breaking Up'. She liked it so much she insisted they take a pause from that track and spend the rest of the session working on this one. "We have an incredible chemistry," said Gwen. "He has so many sides to him. He's so talented, so inspiring. I feel lucky to know him and be able to work with him." A future collaboration from the pair is inevitable.

Pharrell had used studio "down time" – i.e. when waiting for others to arrive for their sessions with him – to hone his tracks. *In My Mind*, after two postponed release dates, finally came out in July 2006. It would, said the artist, allow fans to look inside and see the "real" Pharrell. "The hip-hop songs are more the introspective side of my view and my life, and the R&B stuff is the more vulnerable side." It was to spawn four hit singles. 'Can I Have It Like That' wasn't as successful as hoped, peaking at number 49 in the US, though it made the top three in the UK. *Entertainment Weekly* complained that Pharrell "never puts his hips into it", while *Slant* dismissed it as "curiously inert". (*The Observer* called it a "grinding instant smash".) *Stylus* went so far as to call it "calamitous", while musicOMH slammed Stefani's part as "purely cosmetic, and clearly a transparent means of getting her name on the single to not only boost her own credentials but to help draw Pharrell to the attention of her increasingly mainstream following." 'Angel' was another European hit, while 'Number One' featured fast-rising rapper Kanye West, and a big-budget Hype Williams video. The release of 'That Girl' came across as almost an afterthought.

However, *In My Mind* still made the top three in the States, and went silver. Admittedly, more had been expected from it, given Pharrell's track record, and it was some time before he braved a solo release again. (Of course, when he did, he was an even bigger superstar.) It wasn't as if *In My Mind* lacked star power: other celebrity-pal guests on it included Jay-Z, Nelly and Snoop Dogg. Yet its reception remained lukewarm. "Only so-so," said *Rolling Stone*, "offering a series of modestly tuneful, sometimes snoozy songs." The songs all had "something in common," reckoned *Entertainment Weekly*, "they're not remotely catchy." Ironically, The Neptunes' production on the second Clipse album *Hell Hath No Fury*, released the same year, was hailed as their best in years. Pharrell recorded a remix album of his solo debut – *Out Of My Mind* – with Questlove of The Roots, which, despite gaining no official release, ultimately leaked onto the Internet.

If *In My Mind* had failed to conquer all, it did at least offer gnomic philosophising from Pharrell on its sleeve, a glimpse of strange utterances to come. "Wealth is of the heart and mind, not of the pocket," this very rich man wrote on the back cover. Inside, he added, "What art is to history, time is to space. They are relative and cannot exist without each other. Father Lord, thank you master. Thank you to my family, thank you to my team, and thank you to my fans. Yessurr!"

If the solo music career had experienced a rare (relative) setback, Pharrell was still the boss in other areas. He was at this time happy to be famous, telling MTV that: "It's absolutely bitter, because when I wanted to get in the game they were like 'You dress funny'. I kind of rub it in the face of the naysayers." Now, his fashion sense was drawing attention and winning accolades. Indeed, *Esquire* magazine named him 2005's Best Dressed Man In The World. This was no small-time feat: below him in their list were the likes of George Clooney, Bill Clinton, Donald Trump and Jay-Z. *Esquire*'s fashion editor described those cited as "the most innovative, never-trendy, always perfectly-clad-for-the-occasion individuals who roam the globe as walking examples of what it means to be a man well-clothed." Interviewed by MTV, having posed for the magazine's "style icons" cover with actors Josh Lucas and Luke Wilson, Pharrell shrugged, suggesting that crucially he didn't try too hard. "It's about comfort and flow," he explained. "It's never about whether I'm the best-dressed guy in the room. I never go, 'Oh, I'm killin' 'em tonight!' Things just need to fit naturally. Fashion's more about feel than science." He was to maximize his "feel" into a lucrative side-empire.

One icon who was making a strong comeback at this time was Mariah Carey, whose spectacular *The Emancipation Of Mimi* album, released in 2005, was firing hit singles into the charts deep into 2006. One of these was Neptunes production 'Say Somethin'', which they co-wrote with Mariah and Snoop Dogg. The Paris-set video showed Pharrell and Mariah flirting by the River Seine, while Snoop drawled typically romantic suggestions about which sex acts he'd like to engage in with Mariah in a restroom.

Snoop was genuinely thrilled to "work" with the diva, and thanked Pharrell for bringing it together. "We were working in the same studio," he recalled on *MTV News*. "I was in the front end and she was in the back, and Pharrell actually made it happen. He was like: come down the hallway and get on this mic right now. And Nelly was there too. He gave me direction on which way to take my rap. Despite her reputation as being notoriously hard to please, Mariah's very happy with the results." Snoop, it turned out, had long been a besotted

Mariah fan. "She's so soft. So beautiful, too. I always tell this story: when I was locked up in jail, her first song 'Vision Of Love' was the hottest song in the world. I used to always say, 'Man, if I could meet her! Lord have mercy!'"

The underrated, addictive track itself was called "breezy and playful" by *USA Today*, and the album's "high point" by the *Orlando Sentinel*. Even shooting the video was a "la dolce vita" experience for Pharrell, as he and Mariah played a couple trying to escape the Parisian paparazzi. Initially, actors played the photographer pack, but soon there were so many real paparazzi around that the actors could have been sent home. "That's just a regular day in the life for Mariah, probably," Pharrell told VH1. "I'm a low-key guy, so there's no paparazzi under the studio console or in my apartment, or jumping out of my pool. I'm just not into it. So it's weird when you have these people running up, especially in Paris – they're on Vespas, doing wheelies... it's wild!" He wasn't wrong about Mariah, who knew how to "shake it off", saying, "You know what was so great about being in Paris? Usually I'm inside a hotel room and I don't get to see anything. This time... I got to hang out. I love the electricity this city has. And it gave me a new perspective on this song, which was one of the first I recorded for *The Emancipation Of Mimi*. It's got a hot vibe to it."

America's best-selling album of 2005 also included 'To The Floor' (featuring Nelly), yet another Neptunes credit, on a record primarily produced by Jermaine Dupri. It's also worth noting that that year saw the release – on Star Trak – of Robin Thicke's album *The Evolution Of Robin Thicke*, with The Neptunes producing 'Wanna Love You Girl' (featuring Pharrell). With a Hype Williams video filmed on a remote beach in the Dominican Republic (Pharrell was transported there by plane and boat), it was anticipated that the single would give Star Trak a major hit, but it stalled. Hindsight tells us that the Pharrell-Thicke pairing still had a commercially viable future. There were also outings for Pharrell on LL Cool J's 'Best Dress' (with Jamie Foxx), on Jay-Z's 'Anything' from *Kingdom Come* (with Usher), and the small matter of the Neptunes-produced Beyoncé hit 'Green Light'.

Interviewed by *The Guardian* around this period, Pharrell said he was reading Dan Brown's best-seller *The Da Vinci Code*. "It's about the re-emergence of the Holy Grail," he explained. Asked about his own religious beliefs, he said, "I'm Christian. I ain't been in (to church) for so long, man. But God knows my heart. I have conversations with God a few times every day... I absolutely spend more time thanking him for the shit I don't have than the things I do got." He was asked how he reconciled his enormous wealth with spirituality. "I don't worry about things like that," he said. Later, he added, "I'm a philanthropist, too. I like to think I'd have become some sort of art teacher, or art professor, studying for my PhD. But life doesn't always end up that way. Shit happens. I don't know what might have panned out. I would have been happy. I would have driven a Volvo and married another art teacher." Almost ruefully, he concluded, "When I find my wife, watch what I do."

On another occasion, talking to VH1, he elaborated on his feelings about fame, fortune and romance. "You have to be secure yourself, and know that you will be a good provider for whoever is involved in your life. When you're a musician, there's more to your life than just your music. Chad was fortunate enough to meet his wife years ago and have two beautiful children. I haven't been as fortunate, but there's more to a musician's life than music – family members, friends, things happening. Or things not happening."

Sounds like the man who had everything didn't quite have it all. He didn't have too much longer to wait though...

CHAPTER 8
SEEING SOUNDS

Madonna famously likes to talk about sex, so when her 2008 album *Hard Candy* began with 'Candy Shop', a Neptunes production, liberally scattering around metaphors for sex like "come into my store, I've got candy galore", nobody was too surprised. If anyone knows how to ensure her milkshake brings all the boys (and girls) to the yard, it's our Madge. And she knew which co-write/

production name she wanted too. Pharrell, talking to MTV News about one of his most stellar collaborations yet, said, "We were just in a studio and she was like, 'Look, give me some hot sh*t.'"

Ultimately, Pharrell was involved in no less than seven of the album's twelve tracks, and no longer shared writing credits with Chad Hugo (though he did of course have to share them with Madonna). With the record also featuring heavy contributions from Timbaland and Justin Timberlake, it was another example of the old Virginia Beach crowd's subversive takeover of the chart mainstream. Even if Madonna wasn't as fashionable as she had been, there were still few - arguably no - bigger names in dance and pop.

Pharrell was even to join Madonna onstage for some shows in her Sticky And Sweet world tour. In 2014, however he revealed on an American radio interview that it hadn't always been an easy-going relationship. There were feisty arguments. "The gist of it was that we kept doing this one take over and over," he explained. "And I just saw where it was going. I saw her beginning to get frustrated, so I was trying to get her to deviate from that and just try something different. But she was like: 'I got it!'" Apparently Pharrell told Madonna to change her tone, at which point she suggested they take a break to thrash it out. "We went upstairs and had our little battle. It was cool, and we hugged it out."

Madonna's own recollection of events, in 2008, was slightly different, claiming that Williams reduced her to tears. "I was in a sensitive mood," she told Nightline. "I was singing and I didn't understand the rhythm he wanted me to sing in, and he was kind of giving me a hard time. I was sort of taken aback by the way he was talking to me, so I said, 'Y'know what? We need to talk.' We went upstairs and I said, 'You can't talk to me that way!' And then I just burst into tears. And he was like, 'Oh my God, Madonna has a heart!'I said, 'What?' And I was crying even more."

The pair made up after their spat, and indeed 2015's *Rebel Heart* album sees Madonna collaborating with Pharrell again on 'Back That Up (Do It)'. Pharrell once told Bravo TV that Madonna liked to have the studio "sun-surface hot", indeed so hot that "the walls are sweating". He wasn't complaining, saying it "forces you to pay attention".

Other Pharrell cuts on *Hard Candy* included the Grammy-nominated second single 'Give It 2 Me' (the first was Timbaland's '4 Minutes', on which Madonna duetted with Justin Timberlake). It saw Pharrell guesting in the Tom Munro video, described as "kinky" by the *Daily Mail*. This "thumpy self-empowerment anthem" (*Rolling Stone*) was embraced by some as "unabashedly reviving the celebrative spirit of 'Lucky Star' and 'Holiday', filtering it through hip-hop's sonic boom" (*Entertainment Weekly*). Others, presciently, referenced Nile Rodgers...

Meanwhile Britney Spears' 2007 album *Blackout* revived an old team as The Neptunes produced its closing track 'Why Should I Be Sad?', written by Pharrell. 'I Know' by Jay-Z from *American Gangster* featured Pharrell, and The Neptunes also produced that platinum album's 'Blue Magic'. (Pharrell has also appeared on all three Jay-Z albums – *The Blueprint III*, *Watch The Throne* (with Kanye West) and *Magna Carta Holy Grail* – since then.)

Perhaps the least expected Neptunes productions to date came when they helmed several tracks for Swedish garage-rock band The Hives. The group's *The Black And White Album* came out in late 2007, and made a killing as a source for loud, in-your-face music used by commercials and film trailers. 'Well All Right!' and 'T.H.E.H.I.V.E.S.' were unlikely Neptunes credits. The Swedes were to return the favour by playing on the next N*E*R*D album, *Seeing Sounds*.

Interviewed in London by Ian Gittins for *Man About Town*, Pharrell admitted there was less pressure on N*E*R*D to perform commercially than on some of his other outlets. "Yeah that's the idea," he said. "It's meant for everyone to find their escapism. I want to make music that doesn't require a lot of thought. It makes you think, but doesn't require you to think, or to get it... you know what I mean?"

"When I am producing with The Neptunes, I have no ego," Pharrell continued. "I let that go. I say to the artist, whether it's Beyoncé or Usher, what do you want to do? And when they tell me, I say OK, let's do it like this. It's real simple." He did confess that he hadn't relished the chilly reaction to his solo debut *In My Mind*. "No, I did not enjoy that! It was just too much work. I was all by myself and it is kind of harder when it is your name on the front of the record. Everyone just kept saying: You, you, you! And I was like: No, no no!" After a pause, he told Gittins, "I can promise you now, you won't be getting any more Pharrell solo albums." A hostage to fortune and temptation to fate if ever there was one...

We mentioned Pharrell's synesthesia at the beginning of this book, and the June 2008 N*E*R*D album *Seeing Sounds* claimed this neurological phenomenon (wherein sensory modalities are mixed) as a theme as well as a muse for its title. Centring on a rootsy funk-rock sound, it was described by Chad Hugo as going back to the outfit's roots ("we just want to make people move"), although, increasingly, writing credits were going solely to Pharrell. Chad reported that Williams would arrive at the studio, "ideas in full flower", and lay down a beat and vocal. Hugo would then layer in the extra instrumentation. Pharrell told MTV, "(We) didn't care about genres. We're not doing this for the money. We're doing this for people who pledge allegiance to our movement." Chad seemed worked up, saying, "We had anger, quiet angst. We had something to get off our chest. And we wanted to show we could do it as a band." Perhaps the band they wanted to emulate, curiously, was Limp Bizkit, as Pharrell claimed they wanted to match that band's energy. With this in mind, tight Swedish thrashers The Hives were brought in to play on 'Time For Some Action' and 'Windows', that band's Howlin' Pelle Almqvist singing on the former. Emerging on Star Trak, *Seeing Sounds* – the original working title was N*3*R*D* – was designed as "something that was thought-provoking."

Explaining his synaesthesia and its influence on his lyrics, Pharrell expressed a desire for listeners to be taken on an "emotional rollercoaster" by "this big monster of energy", and a hope that fans would "blast it out" on their speakers. He felt the band had a "renewed purpose", while Chad called it a "big album of LSD, a sonic drug". It intoxicated some, reaching number seven in the States, and winning more positive than negative reviews. PopMatters called it "one of the best genre-blurring club records", praising the production, and *Rolling Stone* found it "experimental and expansive". *The Times* reckoned they were "pushing the boundaries of the popular song". But *The Daily News* slammed Pharrell's vocals, saying "the guy can't sing", while *The Guardian's* Alexis Petridis suggested that the songs being "largely about sex" was "wearisome". The comically-titled, drug-themed lead single 'Everyone Nose (All The Girls Standing In Line For The Bathroom)' was "nicely buffeted electropop" (*Daily Mirror*) and "lampoons party-going cokeheads by sounding like Baha Men after too many rails" (*Pitchfork*). Pharrell stated that he loved the reaction the song got in live concerts, while Shay Haley confided, "Personally, I'm shocked it's being embraced the way it is. I feel it sticks out like a sore thumb in comparison to what you hear every day on the radio... It's just our observation of what we've seen over the last couple of years, so we felt like making a party record out of it." When N*E*R*D played it at The Roundhouse in London, *The Guardian* reported that "Pharrell's knack is connecting with the crowd. Many bands tell the audience they want to party with them, but N*E*R*D seem to mean it."

Pharrell's knack for connecting then saw The Neptunes producing most of Common's Grammy-nominated album *Universal Mind Control*, with Williams guesting on the title track and 'Gladiator'. They also contributed to John Legend's *Evolver* album, producing 'It's Over' with Kanye West. Chad Hugo worked with Ashlee Simpson and Ethiopian-American musician Kenna. Backlash-hawking critics may have been saying The Neptunes' heyday was waning, but the facts show the opposite.

If they'd eased off on the vast numbers of production jobs they'd been taking on, it was because they had nothing to prove. Perhaps more significantly, they were successfully – and lucratively – branching out into other ventures. Their Star Trak label, with the help of their manager Rob Walker, was still doing well, and releasing N*E*R*D's, Pharrell's and Snoop's records, among others. Pharrell explained his business acumen regarding record deals in habitually convoluted terms. "Let's say you get a million dollar deal. Of your full advance the government's taking half in taxes. So right there, it's only a half. That million, you gotta recoup. Recouping with the amount they give you is like trying to fill up a bucket from a barrel with a spoon... it's gonna take a lot of barrels in order for you to make one little bucket, because all you have is a spoon to recoup with."

The Neptunes had always had an eye for the main chance, although – lest we forget – early on not every spin-off idea had worked. Their 2003 straight-to-video movie (which has often been swept under the carpet since), was called *The Neptunes Present...Dude, We're Going To Rio*. A would-be humorous tale of a young man searching for love, it was, said Pharrell at the time, "Unscripted, un-*everything*. It's a walk into our funny, hilarious, ridiculous, stupid, retarded, mindless, insane lives. It's a very candid, sincere perception of us. It's just something for Neptunes fans to go out and buy and see us be stupid. It's really improvisational." Pharrell has since popped up in other films, like *Get Him To The Greek*, and TV shows, like *90210*, but one suspects the icon of style may well not be advertising *Dude, We're Going To Rio* too loudly.

As a burgeoning icon of fashion, despite outbursts to the contrary, the songwriter has branched out with his own clothing labels. In 2005, he'd teamed up with Japanese designer Nigo (of A Bathing Ape) and started Billionaires Boys Club and ICECREAM. (That year *Black Enterprise* magazine named him one of its "most powerful players under 40".) Pharrell fans could buy branded T-shirts, sweatshirts, sneakers, jeans and other items and accessories. "I appreciate what's going on right now," he told *Remix*. "I appreciate my opportunity. So with that opportunity I'm going to get in... I want to break the colour lines. That's the way I grew up."

As well as making money, he was becoming something of an activist, unafraid to state his political views. This wasn't entirely new. Indeed, in 2004 he'd vocally supported the Democrats in the presidential election, wearing a Vote Or Die T-shirt. "I'm not happy because most of the people I've spoken to are not," he told the BBC. "There are more minorities in the States... there were more people who needed Kerry than those who needed Bush. When I did a broadcast with P Diddy encouraging people to vote, I thought how it was the pimps, prostitutes and drug addicts who needed to vote more than those in the suburbs." Pharrell has also supported PETA – People for the Ethical Treatment of Animals – by lending his voice to their answering-machine. "Be kind to animals," he announces.

Advising young people on the potential pitfalls of the music industry, and the importance of education, he said on VH1, "It's not platinum and diamonds and Mercedes. It is business, work, concentration, discipline and understanding... Anybody that wants to get involved with it, do your homework, research it, see what these deals consist of. It's not like you sell two or three million records and never work again. You gotta work really hard. Don't be afraid to go to school and learn about music. It definitely enables you to do more than what they might cookie-cut you out to do. Then learn about the business. Because you don't want to make a good album and then get screwed."

Things continued apace as Pharrell (under his own name, not as half of The Neptunes) produced and guested on 'Kill Dem' for old ally Busta Rhymes's eighth album *Back On My B.S.* "Your traditional Busta and Pharrell combo," Rhymes told MTV. The third album by Virginia Beach rappers Clipse, *Til The Casket Drops*, emerged on Star Trak, most of it produced by The Neptunes. This included the single 'I'm Good', featuring our man. A more high-profile release came in October 2009, when Shakira's *She Wolf* album, which sold two million, included no less than six Neptunes collaborations, like second single 'Did It Again', in which the Colombian star sang of an extra-marital affair.

"I felt very curious and intrigued about the electro-pop world and everything it has to offer," Shakira reported. "I wanted to make sure this album was very bass-y, and that it kicks really hard, and I wanted to concentrate on the beat. But my music, to an extent, is very complex, because I always try to experiment with sounds from other parts of the world." She added, "The title? *She Wolf* is the woman of our time. The woman who knows what she wants and is free of prejudice and preconceived notions. She defends her deepest desires with teeth and claws like a wild animal." Shakira discussed her experience of working with Pharrell. "When collaborating, you always try and capture something from the other person, and I learnt a lot from his method." Revealing that they began four tracks in five days, she observed, "What was interesting is that he's very fast and immediate in the studio, and I'm a little slower."

The sad death of Michael Jackson in June 2009 precipitated an inevitable rush of reissues and remixes of his material. As a lifelong fan who had met The King Of Pop – and handed him the key tracks from *Justified* – Pharrell was better qualified than many to be involved. The Neptunes' remix of The Jackson Five's 'Never Can Say Goodbye' was the second track on that October's *Michael Jackson: The Remix Suite*. Pharrell was also credited as co-writer for the Jennifer Lopez (featuring Pitbull) single 'Fresh Out The Oven', which – being another Neptunes production – sped to number one on the US dance chart. "A typically synth-driven Pharrell beat shows the world," said DJ Booth. Williams also worked on Miami-born Francophile rapper Uffie's debut album, and with Game on his fourth album *The R.E.D. Album*, which he executive-produced. The Neptunes produced Game's 'Mama Knows', (featuring Canadian star Nelly Furtado), who had previously enjoyed great success with Timbaland.

Now, significantly, Pharrell cleverly used his own high-wattage to move into parallel areas, composing (with Heitor Pereira) the soundtrack to computer-animated comedy *Despicable Me*, with Hans Zimmer producing. This summer 2010 blockbuster grossed $543 million worldwide, having cost just $69 million. It launched a franchise, which was to make Pharrell very "happy". "Kids will dig it, adults will smile with amusement," summarised one critic. Pharrell was certainly smiling with amusement when the 2013 sequel came out. Working with the Hollywood Studio Symphony's 67-piece ensemble was presumably also a blast. Robin Thicke sang 'My Life' for the soundtrack album, on a Williams-Thicke co-write.

Pausing only to provide vocals for electronic dance supergroup Swedish House Mafia's hit 'One (Your Name)' – his lyrics were initially intended for a different track – Pharrell now found time to visit his spiritual home turf and engage with the new N*E*R*D album for Star Trak. Released in November 2010, it bore the unpromising title *Nothing*. Arguably more interesting – and something of a curveball – was that Pharrell described it as "a lot of vintage sounds... America meets Crosby, Stills & Nash meets the Moody Blues." And in the single 'Hypnotize U', it gave us a highly important hook-up with French electronica duo Daft Punk. A lucky liaison.

If the video for that track, showing Pharrell hypnotising a group of beautiful women in a mansion, was almost beyond parody in its narcissism, the co-production with Daft Punk was to lead onto great things. Such a shift was welcome, as The Neptunes needed new impetus and fresh stimuli. As *Rave* magazine phrased it, echoing the thoughts of many among the more sceptical, "Pharrell Williams should either stop letting his wang co-write his songs or start giving it a credit."

Nothing reached the outskirts of the Top 20 in the US, launched by the 'Hot-n-Fun' single, with another cameo from Nelly Furtado and another lustful video. Pharrell seemed to think matters were more earnest. "We needed to align ourselves and make ourselves parallel and congruent with what society is feeling," he told *Billboard*. "There's a lot going on and a lot of things people don't necessarily understand. We have a Tea Party. We have conservative Democrats. We have liberals that are nothing like you thought they'd be... So we thought: why not make a timeless album that's kind of a time capsule, so that ten years from now people look at that album and go, 'I remember that era. That's when the *Nothing* album came out.'" It should be noted, too, that Chad Hugo was back on co-writing duties, and the record returned to prioritising digital techniques, despite its psychedelic tinges. Pharrell commented that N*E*R*D's "previous body of work was really good, but to me it wasn't timeless. I didn't feel we were pushing ourselves as much as we could. We needed to perfect the sound, so we kept pushing the date back until it was right..."

No Ripcord reckoned "the album does its best to give certain fans exactly what they want in sexually-driven club grinders, while offering up real, honest-to-goodness substance too. It isn't always a perfect situation, and parts of the album border on forgettable, but when they get it right everything's groovy." *NME* again panned Pharrell's voice: "He continues to labour under the delusion that his cochlea-shredding falsetto sounds like anything other than Prince with his scrotum in a vice." The *Los Angeles Times* wrote, "As the title intimates... there's nothing left in the record bin for the Virginia Beach-bred trio to plunder, having previously dabbled with rock, pop, rap, funk, R&B and electro." MusicOMH simply said, "Not a bad effort, but we've come to expect more."

More, naturally, was what we got, as Pharrell worked with fellow music giants Jay-Z and Kanye West on their massive *Watch The Throne* album, by co-writing and co-producing the cut 'Gotta Have It'. He soon popped up on nu-disco stars Scissor Sisters' album *Magic Hour*, and acclaimed Compton rapper Kendrick Lamar's 'Good Kid'. N*E*R*D supported Damon Albarn's Gorillaz on tour, and Pharrell wrote for Adam Lambert. In January 2012 came a true moment of glory though...

"You're my child with the child from Destiny's Child... the most amazing feeling I feel, words can't describe what I'm feeling, for real..." So quoth a proud Jay-Z in his rap song 'Glory', produced by The Neptunes, and which premiered on his website just two days after his wife Beyoncé gave birth to their first child in January 2012. Daughter Blue Ivy Carter's heartbeat and cries could be heard on the emotional homage (which didn't shirk from discussing the pain the couple had felt over a previous miscarriage), thus making her the youngest person ever to appear on the *Billboard* chart. It even told us all that Blue was conceived in Paris the day before Beyoncé posed for the cover to her album *4*. "Last time the miscarriage was tragic/ We was afraid you'd disappear, but nah baby you're magic." Despite some finding this a case of "too much information", *Time* magazine called it "one of the greatest love songs in hip-hop history". "Just like all those shots of new dads in movies; you can almost smell the cigars being lit," wrote *Village Voice*. In praising its "lilting Neptunes beat", *Rolling Stone*, while comparing it to Stevie Wonder's 'Isn't She Lovely?', reminded us that this was another Pharrell-related triumph. And, revealed a beaming Pharrell, it was, for all its touching candour, to a degree pre-planned rather than entirely spontaneous.

"It was something we had planned before it happened, so we were basically waiting. That was like our nod and homage to when Stevie did it for his baby, Aisha. And we weren't trying to make the same song at all. It was like we wanted to capture a moment in time to commemorate the birth of his baby. I did the same thing with (my son) Rocket: I'm just more quiet and private about my life."

Indeed he was. The glory of fatherhood was something he knew about, but the birth of his own son had been kept fairly hush-hush. "But Jay-Z and his beautiful wife, they live a different lifestyle, and for him it was important for him to stop everything that he had going on and just sort of make a statement to his baby and his wife. I was honoured to be a 'film-maker' for that beat."

Yes, Pharrell was now a father himself, and the media only properly worked it many months after the event. Rocket had been born in 2008 to Pharrell and girlfriend (now wife) Helen Lasichanh. They'd wanted to give the boy a name that might symbolize the success they wished for him in life, and which honoured their favourite musicians. In a major TV interview with Oprah Winfrey, Pharrell revealed: "In the same way that the Indians name their children like after a force or element or animal, we named him after a man-made machine that was meant to ascend. And metaphorically... it was because of, y'know, Stevie Wonder's 'Rocket Love', Elton John's 'Rocket Man' and Herbie Hancock's 'Rock It'. All my favourites. And... his middle name is not 'Man'. It's 'Ayer' after Roy Ayres."

The relationship with model-designer Helen was no whirlwind romance. Pharrell admitted his ego had swollen out of proportion after fame and riches had led him to think it was acceptable to frequently cheat on girlfriends. Meeting Lasichanh however made him realize the error of his roguish ways. Apparently she didn't fall for him straight away, as she was already involved with somebody else. "She didn't answer half my text messages at first," Pharrell told Oprah. "I was like, 'Oh yeah?', because I had that kind of money and reach... I thought I was entitled, and I had to learn that, no, she has a boyfriend and she's not interested." So the pair were "just friends" for over two years. Then Helen became single again, but then Pharrell's "immaturity" (he said) nearly derailed the relationship. "I hurt her a lot in the very beginning once she was free and available, because I had given her all this attention but I wasn't ready to let go (of the bachelor lifestyle). I looked at my life and I was like, 'Man, I could keep doing this for another ten years – is that what I want to do?' And so I made a decision. We made a decision and started dating." Eventually the couple got engaged in 2012, marrying in the summer of 2013, with Rocket five years old.

"He's changed my ways," Pharrell said of his son, boasting of his boy's prowess with technology. "My son teaches me! It's crazy, he teaches me about video games, gadgets..." He added reflectively, "This is one of those times in your life when you're like, 'Think about that one interview when someone asked you a serious question.' And it just hit me.... my answer to you was, 'He teaches me...' That is bizarre to me!" So now we knew what, or rather who, inspired 'Rocket's Theme' on the *Despicable Me* soundtrack.

Of Ethiopian-born Helen, magazines reported that she was "always looking effortlessly stylish" and "statuesque". The wedding surprised even the snooping media, occurring on board a yacht named *Never Say Never* in Miami, Florida in October 2013. Guests included Justin Timberlake, Usher, Busta Rhymes and Robin Thicke. Several of them are reported to have sung, in a "fun mini-concert". The couple asserted their unconventional, bold attitude towards fashion. While she "opted for a navy blue and green checked gown", he "wore a red tartan tuxedo for the occasion". As to the secret of their romance, Pharrell, now 40, reiterated that they were patient best friends first, advising other couples to follow their example. "I'm no relationship expert," he told a New York radio station, "but I just recommend that you get with your 'bestie'. Because y'all agree on everything."

Somehow Pharrell and Helen had managed – and continue to manage – to keep their private life relatively private, despite his immense fame. Asked by interviewer Ian Gittins how he kept the paparazzi and gossip columnists at bay, Pharrell replied, "I take back doors. I lay low. It's not a world I want to be in. I'll let the other artists do that stuff... For me, there are certain aspects of being known that I want, and certain aspects that I don't. My grandmother used to tell me, 'Eat the fish and spit out the bones', and that's how I see it."

Pharrell's also said he likes to "eat cereal" and "hang out in bookstores". "I don't spend a lot, and I certainly don't roll around telling people what I do and what I spend my money on. Those sort of details, and about what I may or may not want in my private life, I really don't talk about. Mostly I'm just working. I'm an Aries and my birthday is on the fifth, and I've been told the number five means somebody who doesn't feel comfortable unless they have twenty million things going on."

He would soon have plenty more going on.

CHAPTER 9
GETTING LUCKY

If anyone thought Pharrell's best years as a hit-maker were behind him, 2013 was the year that proved them spectacularly mistaken. A year that culminated in the release of 'Happy' saw the boy from Virginia Beach involved in two of the biggest pop singles of the modern era – Daft Punk's 'Get Lucky' and Robin Thicke's 'Blurred Lines'.

Just before we get to those, it's worth mentioning that Pharrell had other successes that year, which under normal circumstances would be viewed as enormous. It's just that even work with Jay-Z and with Miley Cyrus got overshadowed by the twenty-first century's most gigantic grooves. For old pal Jay-Z, Pharrell contributed to the *Magna Carta Holy Grail* album, a double-platinum Grammy-winner that shipped a million copies on its first day of release. (He worked on 'Oceans' featuring Frank Ocean, a co-production with Timbaland, and 'BBC', a co-write with Justin Timberlake, among others.)

Miley Cyrus, of course, was the new good-girl-turned-bad provocateur on the pop block. What with The Neptunes' track record with Britney and Mariah, it was no surprise that she craved Pharrell's involvement in her heat-seeking *Bangerz* album, which also hit the number one spot in the US within a week of release. Professionally mouthy Miley compared the record to Michael Jackson's *Bad*, claiming it would "shut everyone up" and "set a new standard for pop music". Britney and Nelly were among the guests, with Pharrell producing '4x4' and '#Get It Right'. Memorably, Miley "twerked" against Robin Thicke's groin at the 2013 MTV Music Awards and ensured she was all anyone talked about. Her performance became the most tweeted-about event in the history of Twitter to date. Amid the storm of much-coveted controversy, Pharrell defended her. "You have to remember this is a 20-year-old evolving," he said in the documentary *Miley: The Movement*. "Her dad is Billy Ray

Cyrus, her godmother is Dolly Parton, and she's raised in the era where hip-hop is king."

Summer 2013 was the era when Pharrell was crowned king again. First in his dancefloor double-whammy came 'Blurred Lines', released 26 March, and a Robin Thicke-Pharrell Williams-Clifford Harris Jr (better known as T.I.) co-write. Produced by Pharrell, and released on Star Trak, it gave the previously comparatively hit-shy Thicke a runaway monster. A number one in the US, UK, and scores of other countries, it became the longest-running American chart-topper of the decade, the fastest digital-seller in history, and the most downloaded track in British history (until it was overtaken by 'Happy'). All well and good until a legal clash with the Marvin Gaye family, who accused the song of copying the "feel" and "sound" of Marvin's classic 'Got To Give It Up', and claims that the lyrics and video were misogynous, which led to a ban in some places.

Prior to the backlash, Thicke had told *GQ* the song was completed in under an hour, saying, "Pharrell and I were in the studio and I was like, 'Damn, we should do something (like 'Got To Give It Up'), with that groove.' Then he started playing a little something and we literally wrote the song in half an hour and recorded it. He and I would go back and forth where I'd sing a line and he'd go 'Hey hey hey!' We started acting like we were two old men on a porch hollering at girls, 'Hey, where you going, girl? Come over here!'" Thicke's manager came up with the idea of making a video that would go viral, claiming, "I knew it would get banned quickly – getting something banned actually helps you." Diane Martel, who had given us the similarly salacious 'Lapdance' video, directed the parade of near-naked models draping themselves over Thicke and Williams.

However, the song was hailed as "one of Pharrell's best beats in years" and a "bubbly bit of disco-shuffling R&B". Thicke replied to the onslaught of subsequent criticism by telling NBC's *The Today Show*, "It's actually a feminist movement within itself. It's saying that men and women are equals as animals and as power." He added that it was about his wife. As for Pharrell, who seemed to swerve most of the flak directed at Thicke, he backed up his pal (who was, of course, signed to his label). He emphasised the line "that man is not your maker", claiming, "I don't know anything that could be more clear about our position in the song... the power is right there in the woman's hand." To *Pitchfork* he complained, "What would be controversial about it? The lyrics are (saying) he (the man) is not God, nor can he produce children, for that matter. What I was trying to say was: 'That man is trying to domesticate you, but you don't need no papers – let me liberate you.' But it was misconstrued. The point is: she's a good girl, and even good girls want to do things, and that's where you have the blurred lines. She expresses it in dancing because she's a good girl. We got a kick out of making people dance, and that was the intention."

A year later, Pharrell told *Stylist* that, "I'm not surprised... that's the way the media works. Anything can be taken out of context, and even though there were models who were topless there... I'm sorry, read the lyrics. I'm talking about the portion that I wrote, not T.I.'s rap." Pharrell regretted nothing, he asserted. "If you know anything about me, and my career, you know how I love women, and the last thing I want to do is degrade". He insisted he'd stand in "whatever boxes I'd like to, as a creative", and added, "Is this really a man's world? Do men give birth to men?"

Robin Thicke's career has since imploded as quickly as 'Blurred Lines' exploded, but once again Pharrell has risen, invulnerable. And with the release of 'Get Lucky' by Daft Punk featuring Pharrell Williams on 19 April, he monopolised the top echelons of pop success. Going on to sell almost ten million copies to date, the song, co-written with the French duo (who produced) and Chic legend Nile Rodgers, won Grammy Awards for Record Of The Year and Best Pop Duo/Group Performance. At the ceremony, Stevie Wonder joined the dream team to perform it onstage.

Pharrell was an ardent Daft Punk fan, having loved even their film soundtracks. "Their trailer for *Tron: Legacy* was amazing," he said. "I was very jealous when I heard that. I told them so to their faces when I saw them. The whole production and mentality that came along with that was amazing."

Leading the promotion for the commercially triumphant album *Random Access Memories*, which itself won three Grammys, 'Get

Lucky' openly embraced its 70s dancefloor influences, most pointedly that of Nile Rodgers himself. He'd already recorded his guitar parts when Pharrell heard about the collaboration from Daft Punk (who he'd previously remixed) "at a Madonna party" and expressed his desire to join in. He joked that he'd be happy to play tambourine. When he came to sing 'Get Lucky', he was interested to find he was required to do multiple takes and repeat certain phrases, as the French pair were perfectionists. "Well, they're robots. Think about it. The very definition of a robot, that's the way they approach everything. Everything is concise, precise, everything is gridded, there are no grey areas for them. I've learned a lot from them. Just not settling. They don't understand settling; they just don't understand that. They believe in doing it two hundred times more than the previous two hundred. But that's why the album is absolutely unbelievable, second to none. Will it change music? I don't know, because music is a funny thing these days. But will it change man? Mankind? And mentality? Absolutely."

Later, Pharrell remarked that he'd aimed for the sense of being "on an exotic island" during a "peachy-coloured sunset". And that the title wasn't about sex but about feeling a fortunate, instant connection with someone.

As the song grew and grew in popularity, Nile Rodgers said, "When I think how it happened... with people who I like a lot... we just decided to go into the studio, and then it turns out like this? It's absolutely remarkable, because no-one was prepared for this. To have this ubiquitous record, that is a hit everywhere, it's amazing to me! I'm out on the road and I can hear it wherever I go. I'm flabbergasted!" 'Get Lucky' became Daft Punk's first British chart-topper (and the year's first million-seller there), and achieved similar soar-away results around the world, from Brazil to Finland, from Spain to Mexico and, of course, the number one position in the US. It was, thought *The Guardian*, "the best thing Pharrell Williams has been involved with for a long time". "Real music to dance to", said BBC Radio One, while the *New York Times*'s Sasha Frere-Jones called it, or specifically Rodgers' performance, "as close to magic as pop comes". For *Rolling Stone* it was a "formidable old-school disco jam", and Norman Cook (Fatboy Slim) said, "It's a breath of fresh (old-school) air... Daft Punk have given us electronic musicians a kick up the arse."

Daft Punk's album saw collaborations with everyone from Giorgio Moroder to Julian Casablancas to Paul Williams to Panda Bear. Pharrell wasn't surprised: "They're hooked into everyone. They just pulled us all together, and I cannot believe that I was a decimal, a comma, in that equation. I'd (gladly) be there just to hold up the equals sign, but I was allowed to be a digit. I cannot believe I was allowed to be even a hyphen in that equation."

As well as singing 'Get Lucky' (a riposte to those who'd ridiculed his vocal style for some years), Pharrell also sang on 'Lose Yourself To Dance', another disco-funk co-write with Nile Rodgers. It was the obvious choice for a follow-up single, but understandably couldn't match the landslide success of its forebear. Pharrell told interviewers he could imagine David Bowie singing it, and it made him feel "like walking down the street in the middle of the night in London, and it's 1984 or 1985... I don't hear Seventies in it at all." The remarkably diverse album was voted the year's finest in many magazine polls, with *Q* saying, "By some margin Daft Punk's best album in a career that's already redefined dance music at least twice. It is, in short, a mind-blower." *Entertainment Weekly* opined, "If EDM (electronic dance music) is turning humans into robots, Daft Punk are working hard to make robot pop feel human again."

Few would deny that an important component of that human touch was Pharrell's voice. Given Daft Punk's carefully-nurtured mystique (and helmets), he was effectively the face of the music too. Finger on the pulse, he welcomed the new breed, or new breeze, in dance. "The idea of collaborating is cool. But I think more than anything I'm just excited about the change, a new wave in music," he told *Rolling Stone*. "There's something happening in the ether, and you know about it or you don't. And if you know, it's because you're probably somewhere engineering the change. If you don't know, then you're probably somewhere missing your call, and you're gonna end up chasing it. The people that are leading are gonna do some really incredible things because they're reaching from oblivion to come up with new stuff. To me, that's interesting to watch. I think the robots are leading. Daft Punk, they're definitely leading."

In fact, so futuristic were Pharrell's sonic taste buds now that he baulked at people calling song-of-the-summer 'Get Lucky' "disco". "I don't know if it's a disco track," he mused on *MTV News*. "If you really think about it, it feels a little bit more 'post-disco'. If you consider all the elements, and where it comes from, that feeling – it kind of feels like it's out of time, like it's not necessarily in a specific time. At least when I hear it." As the track smashed records on streaming sites, he concurred with Nile Rodgers' disbelief. "I thought it would do good, but I didn't know it would be breaking records across the board. I had no idea. It felt great, and it felt different, and you know I live for those types of things, to do things that are different. So the fact that it's been so explosive, and that the people chose to make it the phenomenon it is, the only thing we can say is: thank y'all. I was with the robots yesterday, and, of course, they're super-thankful too."

On another occasion, when asked how he wrote a song, he offered, "I create based on what I feel is missing. You jump in and follow your gut. It's like a sculpture – you're just adding on more clay, you're chiselling away, adding on until you feel it's done. And then you stand back, and go: 'Oh, it's a person!'"

Pharrell Williams: born lucky. And about to get happy.

CHAPTER 10
THE PURSUIT OF HAPPINESS

It may have been tipped by *Rolling Stone* magazine (ahead of its release) to be "an instant contender for 2013's song of the summer", but 'Happy' remains intent on keeping that summer alive for a very long time. Declared the USA's and UK's biggest-selling single of the following year, 2014, and globally ginormous (a chart-topper in twenty-two countries and the *Billboard* chart's champ

of the year to boot), it would be no exaggeration to describe Pharrell's biggest success yet as the feel-good anthem of its era, a cross-generational charmer that has transcended its pop status to become, in certain territories, a political hot potato signifying individuality and freedom.

Not even Pharrell can have imagined it would run and run, crossing both geographical and logical boundaries, as it has. First, the bald facts. Pharrell wrote, performed and produced the song for the soundtrack of the movie *Despicable Me 2*, and it subsequently served as the lead single from his second solo album *G I R L*. He recorded it at Circle House Studios in Miami. The track was officially released on 21 November 2013, along with a memorable long-form video (more of which shortly). It jumped to number one in the States, Canada, New Zealand, Australia, Germany, Ireland, you name it. In the UK it stole the number one spot on a record-breaking four separate occasions, hovering around the higher echelons of the charts for an inordinately long period. American sales have passed six million, and in the UK have reached 1.7 million. With global sales estimated at over ten million, it's made the all-time best-sellers list (and still has some steam left).

It was also nominated for an Academy Award for Best Song, but was controversially pipped to the Oscar by 'Let It Go" from *Frozen*. (Asked afterwards by *GQ* magazine "how badly" he'd wanted the Oscar,

Pharrell wryly replied, "When they read the results, my face was... frozen. But then I thought about it, and I just decided just to... let it go.")

Among its glowing reviews, the most obvious pronounced it "unbelievably catchy" and "the kind of song that makes you want to dance and sing along". Others, like Paul Tingen, making slightly more of an effort, described it as "a mid-tempo soul song in a faux-Motown style, with an arrangement that is, by modern standards, very sparse: programmed drums, one bass and one keyboard part, and handclaps both programmed and played, all topped off by Williams's lead vocals and a whole posse of backing vocals." Those vocals were elsewhere compared to Curtis Mayfield, while the "sprightly neo-soul funk groove" was applauded.

Oddly, Pharrell had nearly given the song away to Cee-Lo Green. After his triumphs with Daft Punk, Pharrell returned from his sessions with them in Paris to meet with Columbia Records company heads. They were greatly enthused by the Daft Punk work, and at this point eager to get 'Get Lucky' out as a single. Planning ahead, they were keen on a new Williams solo album too. Pharrell was delighted, saying later that he was "overwhelmed that someone wanted to know what's in my heart". The announcement of his signing to Columbia was made official in December 2013. In a press release, Columbia chairman Rob Stringer said, "When we excitedly partnered with Pharrell in January this year, we felt it was his time again. Since then, 'Blurred Lines' and 'Get Lucky' have defined pop music in 2013, and now we are preparing to launch Pharrell as a global solo superstar in 2014. 'Happy' is just the beginning."

Having originally penned the song for the 'Crazy' singer, Pharrell at first thought Cee-Lo Green's version was better. But fate intervened, as Elektra, Green's label, decided not to release it, focussing instead on their act's intended Christmas album. Whoops. Pharrell soon realized that all his Christmases had come at once. He described himself as "the luckiest dude there is".

And so 'Happy' became this runaway train, surpassing even the heights of popularity of 'Get Lucky' and 'Blurred Lines'. The man known for facilitating hits for others was now the hit-maker supreme under his own name. In Holland it was number one even before its release. It's now the most successful song in Dutch Top 40 history. In America, March marked its ascendancy to pole position (his fourth number one, but his first as lead artist). It had already passed four million sales by April, and stayed at number one for ten weeks before John Legend's 'All Of Me' finally displaced it. Another long-standing record was broken when it spent fifteen weeks atop the New Zealand charts (beating the 36-year reign of Boney M's 'Rivers Of Babylon').

In Britain, however, 'Happy' took a curiously roundabout journey to all-conquering ubiquity. It climbed the charts for several weeks before becoming the last number one of 2013, on 29 December. It then proceeded, in unorthodox manner, to drop and rise again numerous times. It couldn't be denied. Four times it reclaimed top spot. Only three artists had ever done this, and none since 1957 (!) when Guy Mitchell did so with 'Singing The Blues'. Pharrell's performance at the 2014 Brit Awards gave it another boost. As 'Happy' surged past the one-million sales mark in the UK, statisticians noted it was Williams's third million-seller within a year (after the summer 2013 double-whammy of 'Get Lucky' and 'Blurred Lines'). The only artists in UK history to have achieved this before were The Beatles. And only the Fab Four (with six) and Rihanna (with four) had ever had more than three in a career. 'Happy' was the also first song released in the decade to go three-times platinum in the UK. It's been streamed over 25 million times here.

Now numbers are one thing, but the light-hearted joy spread by the song is less quantifiable. Its video became a cause célèbre of its own. (Though if we may throw in one more number, with over 600 million views on YouTube, it's in the thirty most watched YouTube music-related links ever.) The website 24hoursofhappy.com was launched to present the film, billed as "the world's first 24 hour music video". Directed by Yoann Lemoine, it repeats the four-minute song many times, showing a variety of (happy) people singing (or miming) along while dancing, in the Los Angeles area. Viewers can jump to wherever they like on the timeline.

Pharrell appears at the top of each hour (so, correct, twenty-four times). While most contributors are not "famous", celebrity cameos come from a broad spectrum. Among these: Steve Carell (associated with *Despicable Me 2*, of course), Jimmy Kimmel, Magic Johnson, Jamie Foxx, Ana Ortiz, Kelly Osbourne, Sergio Mendes, Odd Future, Miranda Cosgrove (also from the film), and JoJo. In the scene at 3am, Pharrell dances with the "minions" from the movie – in a cinema where the film is playing.

The "single" edit of the video was nominated at the MTV Video Music Awards 2014 as Best Male Video and Video Of The Year. It may not have won, but it wasn't as if Pharrell could be too downhearted, given the roll he was now on. The video even spawned "cover" versions, around the world. Controversy was caused in both Armenia and Albania, as the theme was appropriated for protest gestures.

Yet the most incendiary "cover video" of all emerged from Iran. A group of dancing fans who'd created a tribute video to 'Happy' there were distinctly unhappy when they were arrested by police. The song represented "vulgarity", a police chief stated, and "hurt public chastity"; the video was "obnoxious". The females were not wearing veils. Iranian police reportedly told the ISNA news agency: "After a vulgar clip which hurt public chastity was released in cyberspace, police decided to identify those involved in making that clip. Our dear youths should try to avoid these kinds of people. Like actors, singers, and these kinds of problems. Try to avoid it."

There was an outcry around the world, and subsequently the Iranian president – scenting a PR disaster – distanced himself from the arrest, tweeting that "Happiness is our people's right. We shouldn't be too hard on behaviours caused by joy." The dancers – and the video's director – were released. However, it was reported in *The Guardian* on 19 September 2014 that seven of the dancers in the video (shown dancing merrily on Tehran rooftops and throughout the streets) had been given suspended sentences of ninety-one lashes each and potential jail sentences if they commit another "crime" within three years.

According to the International Campaign for Human Rights, a New-York based non-profit organisation, a Tehran court had found the group guilty of conducting "illicit relations". The seven had to go on Iranian television and confess to their "crimes", allegedly under duress. "This is unfair: imprisonment and lashes – for what?" tweeted an Iranian supporter. Another added, "Don't be happy in Iran; otherwise you'll be seen as having illicit relations."

It's an indication of the power of pop music to move, and its power to lift the spirit: something most of us, perhaps, take for granted. And Pharrell himself posted in support of the daring dancers on his Facebook page: "It is beyond sad that these kids were arrested for trying to spread happiness."

Elsewhere, thankfully, the happiness was still being wantonly spread. The track appeared in ads for Beats by Dr .Dre and car manufacturer, Fiat. It was covered by Gwyneth Paltrow on the hundredth episode of TV show *Glee*, and on *The X Factor* and *The*

Voice in the US. Talk show host Jimmy Fallon even embarked on a duet with one Sarah Palin (while impersonating Vladimir Putin). And just to confirm that 'Happy' had reached peak familiarity in every household, it received the ultimate accolade – a Weird Al Yankovic version, dubbed 'Tacky'.

The *Los Angeles Times* profiled Pharrell at the peak of 'Happy'-mania, or rather during the first phase of its world domination. He was working simultaneously then, in a Melrose Avenue studio complex, on mixing his album *G I R L*, and on scoring *The Amazing Spider-Man 2*, with Hans Zimmer. Pharrell confirmed that he'd modelled 'Happy' after Curtis Mayfield, and that the song's "cheery gospel-funk" was intended, in *Despicable Me 2*, to "humanize" the grumpy villain Gru (as voiced by Steve Carell). The head of Illumination Entertainment, who made both *Despicable Me* films for Universal Pictures, chipped in that, "When you look at the history of songs written for films, the ones that have broken out to have a meaningful life beyond the films are very rare. There's an infectious quality to 'Happy' that just resonates."

Pharrell was at this stage on the Oscar campaign trail, with 'Happy' up against U2's 'Ordinary Love' from *Mandela: Long Walk To Freedom* and the aforementioned eventual winner, 'Let It Go', sung by Idina Menzel in Disney's *Frozen*. He put a shift in, doing early-morning TV show slots (wearing the Westwood hat that had become his trademark since the Grammys in January), attending Oscar nominees' lunches at the Beverly Hilton, performing 'Happy' at the NBA All-Star game, and at the Brit Awards in London. On the Oscars show he did it again. "This is probably the most I've ever been humbled in my entire life," he said of the global response to his song. "Because it's something bigger than me, bigger than anything I've ever done."

Quite a statement given his track record of success. This high profile wasn't harming the prospects of his second solo album, *G I R L*, of course, and its release date was set for the day after the Oscars. Pharrell offered, at this early stage, that "the criteria was that I wanted it to feel festive and celebratory." The head of Columbia Records, Ashley Newton, added that, "*G I R L* exudes a confidence that (Pharrell) might not have had previously." For instance, suggested a journalist, such as when he released "his first solo disc, 2006's *In My Mind*, which sold fewer than half a million copies and earned lukewarm reviews." Newton was more positive. "All his moves are so right at the moment," he said. "He's someone who can feel his own creativity swirling around, and that just changes a person's demeanour." Singing star Jennifer Hudson joined in the praise. "Pharrell always brings such an amazing energy to whatever he's working on." (He'd latterly worked on her recent single 'I Can't Describe (The Way I Feel)', as well as Miley Cyrus and Beyoncé tracks... no wonder he won the Grammy for Producer Of The Year.) "When I hear one of his songs," Hudson gushed, "I'll be like: why am I feeling so good? Oh – because it's a Pharrell track!" And there, Jennifer Hudson puts her finger on something. The world heard 'Happy'. It was a Pharrell track. The world felt good.

The song's coronation was confirmed in December 2014 when the inaugural BBC Music Awards took place at London's Earls Court. There were only three awards up for grabs, but Pharrell took two of them (despite being in L.A., and not attending the BBC's high-profile ceremony), while 23-year-old singer-songwriter Ed Sheeran took the third (Best British Artist) thanks in no small part to collaborating with him. (Sheeran performed live the Williams-produced hit 'Sing'.) As well as screening live across the UK, the show was transmitted in America, Japan, Denmark and Ireland.

Pharrell won both Best International Artist and Song Of The Year (for 'Happy', naturally), the latter category having been decided by a public vote among Radio One and Radio Two listeners. Actor Idris Elba announced that one. Pharrell was shown via a live feed being presented with both awards by friend and glamorous co-worker Gwen Stefani. (They were filming the US version of *The Voice*.) He praised both Stefani and Sheeran, adding, "How amazing it is to have a song that is considered among all of the other really, really great songs. As writers and producers we are beholden to what the audience thinks and what you guys want to do, so when you say 'Song of the Year', really it's not my award, it's your award."

He called the sweeping popularity of 'Happy' "weird" and "not something I can determine". On a night when as well as Sheeran, such luminaries as Take That, One Direction, Coldplay, Clean Bandit, Ella Henderson, Labrinth, Gregory Porter, Tom Jones and Paloma Faith performed, it was the absent Pharrell's night. "It's been an amazing experience and a great journey, thanks to the BBC and countless amazing English fans, who have lifted me to unimaginable heights."

Not everybody was thrilled, as the *Mirror* reported that "fans were a little disappointed with who picked up the prizes." This though seemed to be based on a handful of tweets, one of which said: "So basically they have given away two awards to Pharrell Williams who isn't there? The point is?" There was also disgruntlement, the newspaper added, that he'd thanked "English" and not "British" fans. Yet as International Artist, Pharrell had won a category where the fellow nominees were top-rank: Prince, Taylor Swift, Dolly Parton, Lorde and Gregory Porter. He probably recovered any lost ground in declaring that, "The UK has always been amazing to me and so many other artists who just want to do different things." 'Happy' would not, could not, be stopped.

CHAPTER 11
CELEBRATION

"Women are a phenomenal force in my life and my career... the cornerstone of existence," Pharrell told a room of journalists at a playback of the *G I R L* album. He saw a future, where "75 per cent of the world is run by women... that's going to happen, and I want to be on the right side of it." Some thought he was over-compensating for the 'Blurred Lines' furore (it was now routinely being labelled "the most controversial song of the decade"); others just wanted to hear Motown-styled melodies to match 'Happy'. Pharrell's first solo album for eight years was a lot lighter and poppier than *In My Mind*, and a "celebration" of women, albeit one with a sleeve portraying him as, not for the first time, a ladies' man, and dodgy sexual-metaphor lyrics that promoted that notion. "You can't deny that this is the sound of an artist thoroughly enjoying himself," said *The Guardian*'s four-star review. "Sometimes that's the most important message of all."

Pharrell's statement upon its release read, "When Columbia Records presented me with the opportunity to make an album (after the success of 'Get Lucky'), three things came to mind. One was the sense of overwhelming honour that I felt when I realized they were interested in partnering with me on the album that I had always dreamed of making. Two, it would have to feel festive and urgent. And three, I instantly knew it would be called *G I R L*. I hope you like it." Asked about the double-spacing of the title, he told Zane Lowe, "Because when you look at it, it looks a little weird... because society is a little unbalanced."

Released on 3 March 2014, *G I R L* emerged on the iamOTHER label, which Pharrell had launched (with Columbia) in 2012. Adding to all his other business interests, iamOTHER has been summarised as "a multi-media creative collective", which "serves as an umbrella" for his Billionaire Boys Club and ICECREAM clothing lines, his Bionic Yarn textile company, and his own YouTube channel, which focuses on music, art and fashion. "A cultural movement dedicated to thinkers, innovators and outcasts," said Williams. It's shown original series such as *Awkward Black Girl*, documentaries, style tips and celebrity hip-hop interviews.

The Grammy-nominated album's guests were drawn from the top-rank of Pharrell's extensive contacts book, like Justin Timberlake, Alicia Keys, Daft Punk, Miley Cyrus, Kelly Osbourne, Hans Zimmer and Timbaland. And yet it was Pharrell's own falsetto, once mocked, which dominated the slinky grooves and their flecks of PM Dawn. *G I R L* reached number one in twelve countries, including the UK. It was thwarted at number two in the US, but has sold well over half a million there. With 'Happy' proving such a once-in-a-generation hit, the follow-up singles struggled to raise comparable heat, but "Marilyn Monroe" sang of "helpless romantics" while name-checking Cleopatra and Joan Of Arc, 'Come Get It Bae' featured Cyrus and motorbikes-as-sex double entendres, 'Gust Of Wind' was another Daft Punk collaboration, and 'It Girl', with its wild guitar lines, had an anime video showing Pharrell as a variety of Japanese cartoon-and-game characters. 'Brand New' was a snappily rhythmic duet with old cohort Timberlake, while 'Know Who You Are' a soulful team-up with Keys.

"A relentlessly positive and unselfconsciously joyful tour de force," said *Billboard*, while *Spin* mentioned its "lighter-than-helium vibe, the most audacious milestone in the Neptunes/N*E*R*D icon's already storied career." *Time Out* reckoned, "The best you can say is that Pharrell has created, hands-down, one of the biggest and best pop albums of the year. The worst you can say is that it sometimes sounds a bit Magic FM. Oddly age-appropriate, in fact, for one so young-looking."

Presumably keeping busy – on top of (or underneath) that trademark Vivienne Westwood hat – is what keeps Pharrell so young-looking as he dives into his forties. As well as *G I R L* and the *Despicable Me 2* soundtrack (and chipping in with Hans Zimmer on the *Man Of Steel* score), there was work with Frank Ocean, Major Lazer, Future, Azealia Banks and that Ed Sheeran mega-hit, 'Sing'. Sheeran confessed that Justin Timberlake's hits were "pretty close to a direct inspiration. I love *Justified*… so took from those." "While Pharrell's influence is writ large," wrote *The Guardian*, "there's enough of Sheeran there to prevent it coming across as horrible pastiche." The puppet-based video led to Sheeran and Pharrell winning the Best Male Video award at 2014's MTV Music Video Awards. Pharrell had also produced the aforementioned Jennifer Hudson track 'I Can't Describe (The Way I Feel)', which she'd performed with T.I. on the Soul Train awards alongside dancefloor legends Chaka Khan and Evelyn "Champagne" King. He was of course working with Gwen Stefani again, and he'd co-written and produced 'Can't Rely On You' for British star Paloma Faith. Reportedly the pair met at New York's Metropolitan Museum Of Art Met Ball, and Pharrell approached Faith, tapped his phone number into her mobile and, to her delight, added, "I'm ready to work."

Seems he always is. Outside of music – and the Dear G I R L tour – he continued to expand his extra-curricular empire, curating an art show (also named *G I R L*) in Paris at the Gallerie Perrotin. It included artists like Marina Abramović and Takashi Murakami. He developed a unisex fragrance with Comme Des Garçons. He's designed jewellery and glasses for Louis Vuitton, and furniture with Emmanuel Perrotin and Domeau & Pérès. He's partnered with Adidas and G-Star Raw for various deals, and released a collection for Uniqlo.

And, still branching out, he published a lavishly illustrated coffee-table book, *Places And Spaces I've Been*, "an insight into the synergetic process which has brought the artist such success". It looked at his indomitable musical career and collaborations but also his other creative pursuits, and saw Pharrell himself interviewing everyone from Jay-Z to *Vogue* figurehead Anna Wintour, from astronaut Buzz Aldrin to Kanye West. Complex.com praised his "intellectual curiosity", while the *New York Journal of Books* spoke of his "experimental and multimodal meditation on contemporary cultural context and its implications... with an eclectic A-list cast." "One of our time's most innovative figures... redefining culture for an entire generation," gushed *Plastik* magazine.

All in all, not bad for someone who has described his school-days self as "the class clown, just kinda talkative". His brother, David, once told the press Pharrell hadn't changed at all since becoming a superstar. "He keeps it simple." Certainly his masterstroke as a producer had been to strip things down, a kind of "anti-Phil Spector", but his varied musical upbringing had also played a part, perhaps subconsciously. As a child, Pharrell recalled, "the music I was accustomed to, from the radio, was Queen, then Michael Jackson, then Stevie Wonder, then Genesis, then Madonna..." From Afrika Bambaataa to Daft Punk, from Eddie Kendricks to Donald Fagen (*The Nightfly* is one of his favourite albums), he'd listened, learned, and lithely utilised.

An open mind can be a pulsing, productive thing. "*Star Trek* is incredible because it reminds us that there is so much more out there!" he enthused to Ian Gittins. "Carl Sagan, who was a genius, said that our solar system – not our planet, but our solar system – is but one grain of sand on the beach of existence, and I truly believe that. Think about it – our solar system with its planets is just one of a trillion solar systems in a little sector of the boondocks of the Milky Way. One of a trillion! So even if we forget everything outside of that, that is nine trillion planets. And people really think we are the only life? The sheer numbers tell us we can't be the only life form! The problem is there are these huge distances between these solar systems so no living species can make it that far, unless they can harness the technology of wormholes..."

Back on Earth, Captain Pharrell has told *GQ* of his religious views – "On paper I'm a Christian, but really I'm a Universalist" – and said of those who dismiss the possibility of the existence of God, "That's so incredibly arrogant and pompous. It's amazing that there are people who really believe that." His own philanthropic good deeds are indisputably praise-worthy, as he is currently funding the building of a $35-million afterschool space in his Virginia Beach hometown. (His charity From One Hand To AnOTHER is a foundation formed for helping youths between the ages of 7-20 who are in "at-risk communities" nationwide.) Designed by Chad Oppenheim of Miami's Oppenheim Architecture and Design, the Pharrell Williams Resource Centre aims to "make the world a better place," says the designer. "Pharrell had a unique experience growing up with a local educator that gave him the confidence to pursue his talents, and he wants to provide the same atmosphere for future generations." The man himself has stated, "I believe the architecture of a building says a lot about its soul, and I wanted a building for the centre that makes a statement to the world and the kids, something that will stand as a monument of optimism... to look like something out of the future, so it will inspire the kids in it to aspire to greater things."

There's aspiration aplenty on TV series *The Voice*, and Pharrell joined the coaching panel on the hit American version in September 2014, alongside good friend Gwen Stefani, Adam Levine (of Maroon 5) and country star Blake Shelton. Such luminaries as Usher, Shakira, Cee-Lo Green and Christina Aguilera have coached on previous seasons. Pharrell has already brought in Alicia Keys, Taylor Swift and Diana Ross as his "advisors". That contacts book of his really is quite something. Never one to miss a main chance, he and Stefani had also linked up to write 'Shine' for the *Paddington* movie. "What a wonderful opportunity, as a parent, to contribute to something as classic, authentic and generational to all our lives as Paddington Bear," said Pharrell. The Williams-Stefani pairing also performed their new collaboration 'Spark The Fire' on *The Voice* in December 2014, and Pharrell signed on for the eighth series, though Christina Aguilera will return to replace Stefani. Still, Pharrell's tearful yet jubilant interview as his successes were lionised on *The Oprah Winfrey Show* remains probably his TV pinnacle.

On top of the world, spectacularly successful, relentlessly delving into new areas, Pharrell is indeed, as he phrased it himself, "mega-mega fortunate". Yet it's an indication of his drive that he still feels he has a way to go. "The funny thing is, I still don't think I made it there!" he's said recently. "I don't even know if I'm halfway. I think I'll know when I get there, but I'm nowhere near. I see what I can do, and I realize that my performance could be so much better. Lyrically, I could be so much sharper. Melodically, I could be so much stickier. Musically, I could have so much more texture. So I'm constantly trying to find new ways to mix things up..."

Millions of fans around the solar system are more than happy to go on witnessing and relishing the results. In 2015 Pharrell's train just kept on running...

CHAPTER 12
THE END?

In a life of limitless victories, there was one thing Pharrell didn't win. In December 2015, Season 9 of America's *The Voice* was won by coach Adam Levine's singer Jordan Smith. Undeterred, Pharrell signed up for Season 10, his fourth, opening on February 29, 2016. Christina Aguilera returns as a coach, replacing Pharrell's pal Gwen Stefani. His "advisor" for the new season will be P. Diddy.

In every other area, Williams was still appearing triumphant. The year 2015 had begun with a major announcement. Pharrell teamed up with no less a figurehead than former Vice President of the USA and environmental campaigner Al Gore to reveal plans for a super-scale Live Earth concert. Aiming to raise global awareness about the inconvenient truth of climate change, this Live Earth show (or group of shows, across continents) – of which Pharrell was musical director – made front page news everywhere. The date of June 18 was declared Live Earth day, with concerts planned on all seven continents – including Antarctica. As things turned out, the plan was later postponed, but as 2015 dawned the odd couple of Williams and Gore were brimming with hope and enthusiasm.

They spoke at the World Economic Forum in Davos, predicting a global TV audience of two billion, across 193 networks. Said Pharrell, "Instead of just having people perform, we literally are going to have humanity harmonise all at once." Recalling playing a Live Earth concert in Rio de Janeiro in 2007, he said, "(It was) a ball, but... you would have pundits and comedians who didn't understand global warming, and we were often ridiculed. We want to do something very different this time." He'd previously donated frequently to the Alliance for Climate Protection, and nobody doubted that his heart was in the right place. Al Gore, of course, brought tremendous credibility in this area. Producer Kevin Wall added, "The power of music is unique because it's borderless, without language. Pharrell will use that power.

When you combine music with a message, you can effect change."

Sadly, in May, a down-sizing in the dreamed-of project's scope, pitched as a "delay", was announced. The big and idealistic aspirations of Pharrell and Gore had to be modified. This "shift in timing" meant that a free concert in Paris in the autumn was now the plan. Live Earth's statement said this would "best reflect the global demand for climate action", adding, "We are excited to announce that this allows us to host a free, public concert, featuring countless artists ... we'll host an event which transcends social and cultural barriers, matches the scale of the challenge we face, and enables us to maximise our impact on the issue."

Yet even in November 2015, when the show at last got going, the harshness of the modern world intruded. Al Gore was anchoring a 24-hour webcast from a studio at the foot of the Eiffel Tower; its title *24 Hours Of Reality And Live Earth*. Reality rather dominated, as the Paris terrorist attacks caused carnage in the city and shocked the world. Gore expressed his condolences on air, and suspended this scaled-down Live Earth. "Out of solidarity with the French people and the city of Paris, we have decided to suspend our broadcast," he announced. "Our thoughts are with all who have been affected and the entire nation of France." Duran Duran had played outside the Eiffel Tower at 6.30pm, and the bill – now called off – was to feature the A-list names of Bon Jovi, Elton John and Pharrell himself. It was a chastening end, or at least pause, to Williams's Live Earth dream, but nobody would put it past him to get the idea up and running again in the future.

On a considerably lighter note, Pharrell was now so well-known a figure that in February 2015 he'd appeared in a cameo in *The Simpsons*, Season 26, Episode 13. That's when you know you've arrived! The episode 'Walking Big And Tall' featured the star coming to Springfield to write a new anthem for the town. The yellow-centric animated citizens gave the celebrity short shrift, as is their custom.

Bouncing buoyantly back, Pharrell shone at the 2015 Grammy Awards, performing an extended orchestral version of 'Happy' with composer Hans Zimmer and pianist Lang Lang. He incorporated a topical tribute to the Black Lives Matter movement, inspired by Eric Garner's death and the incendiary events in Ferguson, Missouri.

He'd also won Best International Male Solo Artist at the Brits in February, beating off fellow nominees Beck, Hozier, Jack White and John Legend. Of course he'd closed the previous year's ceremony with a performance of 'Get Lucky', 'Happy' and 'Good Times' with Chic man Nile Rodgers. This year he was content just to receive his award – his first from The Brits. It was remarked upon in some quarters that he was the only non-white winner that year. He kept up his love affair with the country by appearing to great acclaim at both the Isle of Wight Festival and the Glastonbury Festival.

He was also finding time for in the studio. 'Freedom!' gave him another popular success. Released for streaming by Apple Music in June, its video subsequently won a Grammy nomination for Best Music Video. "An awesome track with a feel-good vibe and a positive message," said *MusicSnake*'s reviewer. "The lyrics are uplifting and promote living a happy life without restrictions or limitations." Textbook Pharrell. Its chart showing was modest because of its (in some regions) streaming-only status but it still went platinum in Italy!

From (Al) Gore to *Bush*: perhaps Pharrell's most effective studio work of this period was his production on Snoop Dogg's thirteenth album. Some called it a return to what he does best. *Bush* came out on May 12, and topped the R&B/Hip Hop albums chart. Pharrell was assisted by "additional production" from old Neptunes pal Chad Hugo, and the winning combo of he and Snoop attracted a who's who of guest stars. Kendrick Lamar, Gwen Stefani, T.I., Rick Ross and Charlie "The Gap Band" Wilson (on first single 'Peaches 'n' Cream') were joined by no less an icon than Stevie Wonder. Stevie's irresistible harmonica could be heard on the album's opener 'California Roll'.

It wouldn't be Snoop without controversy, and 'So Many Pros', the second single, attracted its share. Originally a Timbaland track, now reworked by Pharrell with himself, Chad Hugo and Justin Timberlake on backing vocals, its title was at first 'So Many Hoes'. Snoop revealed on the BBC's *Graham Norton Show* that it was Pharrell who had persuaded him to adopt a less provocative – some might say outdated – title for the track. Its video, directed by Francois Rousselet, went on to win the 2015 MTV Video Music Award for Best Art Direction.

The *Bush* album drew enthusiastic reviews, with the *Los Angeles Times* suggesting, "There aren't many 90s rappers who could credibly settle into a sound like this". *The Guardian* called it "a high five of an album, made for hydraulic cars and throbbing dancefloors". Emphasising its frequent use of retro fittings, *Rolling Stone* considered it "a pleasant stroll down memory lane".

Pharrell however was still bossing the present. Expanding his business interests still further, he entered the world of children's books, with an adaptation of 'Happy'. While gaining an exclamation mark, it showed photographs of children of different cultures across the world demonstrating what it meant to them to be happy. The author's note encouraged kids to be "happy helpers". *Publishers Weekly* was among those to grin along: "The expressive outfits and giant smiles the children wear are beyond infectious, and the homespun nature of the props and set-ups (a group of rockers plays on cardboard instruments, not Fender guitars) makes the book feel like a celebration of kids being kids." "It's a perfect addition to any child's bookshelf and any classroom library," agreed *The Examiner*. "We should all spread some of the happiness that can be found between the covers of this special picture book."

More happiness was spread around Pharrell's aura as his big deal with Adidas began to bear fruit. His trainers were colourful to say the least. The Adidas x Pharrell "Supercolor" Superstar collection arrived and redefined the rainbow. "Supercolor is a celebration of equality through diversity", ran some of the promotional material. "With fifty colours of the Superstar, everybody will be able to select his or her colour. More diverse, therefore more individual... all colours are equal. Choose your colour." Adidas beamed, "Pharrell Williams knows that the most empowering thing you can give a superstar is the freedom of expression."

These successes would have countered, to a degree, the less happy moment Pharrell experienced when the long-standing issues with Marvin Gaye's family regarding 'Blurred Lines' came to a head. A jury determined unanimously that the 2013 Robin Thicke hit song was an infringement of Gaye's 1977 hit 'Got To Give It Up'. They awarded the Gaye family $7.4 million in damages for copyright infringement based on profits generated. Williams and Thicke announced their intention to appeal, and the verdict was questioned by everyone from Nile Rodgers and John Legend to Keith Urban and Weird Al.

Pharrell shook it off and savoured some good news. In October the Tisch School of the Arts at New York University named him as their artist-in-residence. The same month, he announced that he'd perform in November at Emanuel AME Church in Charleston, South Carolina, where nine black people had been shot in June. The televised show, with a gospel choir, was aiming to foster race relations. It took the name Shining A Light: a concert for progress on race in America.

He evidently wasn't afraid of the big stages. In March he'd addressed the UN, telling those present that "happiness is your birthright". The United Nations' International Day of Happiness released a video, through Secretary General Ban Ki-Moon, asking everyone to share the song which makes them smile. (A simultaneous report ranking countries in order of happiness placed Denmark top, with Europe dominating the top ten, so Pharrell still had work to do in America.) The musician also asked people to send in their pictures and videos of themselves dancing to 'Happy', and chose the best ones.

Furthermore he used the occasion to again promote climate change awareness, urging everyone to sign Live Earth's petition asking global leaders to adopt a new climate agreement. He made an exclusive mix tape for Internet radio service Pandora to draw attention to the movement. (On it, with the assistance of Ed Sheeran, John Legend, David Guetta, James Blunt, Charlize Theron and others, he placed tunes from Daft Punk, Michael Jackson, Kanye West, Fleetwood Mac, Missy Elliott, Ray Charles, Weezer and many more.) "In a year where there is so much turmoil in the world, from social conflict to climate change, we need moments to stop and celebrate happiness," he declared in a statement. "Protecting our planet is fundamental to the pursuit of human happiness and that is why we have chosen to support Live Earth's movement to raise a billion voices for climate action. We believe that happiness can change the world."

He made the fashion papers happy at the 2016 Oscars ceremony simply by turning up without any socks. "After shocking crowds in his shorts recently," ran one report, "he's arrived this time with his ankles on full display." What an outrage! Pharrell, now 42, walked the red carpet in rolled-up trousers – sockless – with his wife Helen.

The 88th Academy Awards were held at the Dolby Theatre in

Hollywood on Sunday 28 February, and hosted by comedian Chris Rock. There was controversy this year over the scarceness of black nominees, and Rock made constant reference to this in his onstage quips. Pharrell's focus however was on honouring one of music's all-time greats, as he and another of his heroes, Quincy Jones, presented the Oscar for Best Original Score (for the Quentin Tarantino film *The Hateful Eight*) to no less legendary a figure than Ennio Morricone. If anyone was overdue an Oscar, it was the 87-year-old Italian composer. Quincy Jones had previously told the press that he'd use the opportunity to talk about diversity. "They called me to go present, with Pharrell and Common," he'd said. "When I'm there in Los Angeles I'm going to ask them to let me speak for five minutes on the subject. If not, I'm not going to present." It seems an alternative agreement was settled, however, as on the night he didn't bring the matter up, perhaps because so many others already had.

For his part, Pharrell looked both slick and relaxed in a tuxedo and blonde-dyed short hair, smiling when Jones referred to soundtrack music as "motion lotion".

While Live Earth may have encountered some obstacles to its ambition, Pharrell just keeps on climbing, making sure the world isn't short on motion lotion. Nobody doubts that this sensitive superstar will continue to come up with fresh ideas and fine music over the coming years. He really does believe that happiness can change the world, and he's doing his level best to spread it around. Clap along.

DISCOGRAPHY

From producer/songwriter credits on other artists' records to writing, recording, producing and releasing his own material, as well as featured collaborations with famous friends, guest appearances on songs, writing children's books, arranging and composing film scores and mentoring upcoming singers on TV shows such as The Voice in the United States, Pharrell Williams' schedule has been beyond busy since around the year 2000.

This is a comprehensive discography of almost everything Pharrell has released to date as a solo artist and collaborator. Proof, should it be needed, that the multi-talented musical pioneer and innovator's commitment to working hard has paid off in a big way...

THE NEPTUNES

ALBUMS

The Neptunes Present... Clones (2003)

SINGLES

'Frontin'' (featuring Jay-Z, 2003)

'Light Your Ass on Fire' (featuring Busta Rhymes, 2003)

'It Blows My Mind' (featuring Snoop Dogg, 2003)

'Hot Damn' (featuring Clipse, 2003)

(N*E*R*D)

ALBUMS

In Search Of...(2002)

Fly or Die (2004)

Seeing Sounds (2008)

Nothing (2010)

SINGLES

'Lapdance' (featuring Lee Harvey and Vita, 2001)

'Rock Star' (2002)

'Provider' (2002)

'She Wants to Move' (2004)

'Maybe' (2004)

'Everyone Nose (All the Girls Standing in the Line for the Bathroom)' (2008)

'Spaz' (2008)

'Sooner or Later' (2009)

'Hot-n-Fun' (featuring Nelly Furtado, 2010)

'Hypnotize U' (2010)

SOLO ARTIST

ALBUMS

In My Mind (2006)

The Billionaire Boys' Club (EP, 2012)

Pink Slime (EP with Mac Miller, 2013)

Girl (2014)

SINGLES

'Show Me Your Soul' (with P. Diddy, Lenny Kravitz and Loon, 2003)

'Can I Have It Like That' (featuring Gwen Stefani, 2005)

'Angel' (2006)

'Number One' (featuring Kanye West, 2006)

'That Girl' (featuring Snoop Dogg and Charlie Wilson, 2006)

'Happy' (2013)

'Marilyn Monroe' (2014)

'Come Get It Bae' (2014)

'Gust of Wind' (featuring Daft Punk, 2014)

'It Girl' (2014)

'Freedom' (2015)

COLLABORATION AS FEATURED ARTIST

'I Just Wanna Love U (Give It 2 Me)' (Jay-Z featuring Pharrell, 2000)

'Formal Invite' (Ray J featuring Pharrell, 2002)

'Pass the Courvoisier, Part II' (Busta Rhymes featuring P. Diddy and Pharrell, 2002)

'Boys' (Britney Spears featuring Pharrell, 2002)

'When the Last Time' (Clipse featuring Kelis and Pharrell, 2002)

'From tha Chuuuch to da Palace' (Snoop Dogg featuring Pharrell, 2002)

'Beautiful' (Snoop Dogg featuring Pharrell and Charlie Wilson, 2003)

'Excuse Me Miss' (Jay-Z featuring Pharrell, 2003)
'Belly Dancer' (Kardinal Offishall featuring Pharrell, 2003)
'Light Your Ass on Fire' (Busta Rhymes featuring Pharrell, 2003)
'Change Clothes' (Jay-Z featuring Pharrell, 2003)
'Drop It Like It's Hot' (Snoop Dogg featuring Pharrell, 2004)
'Let's Get Blown' (Snoop Dogg featuring Pharrell, 2004)
'Wanna Love You Girl' (Robin Thicke featuring Pharrell, 2006)
'Margarita' (Sleepy Brown featuring Big Boi and Pharrell, 2006)
'Mr. Me Too' (Clipse featuring Pharrell, 2006)
'Money Maker' (Ludacris featuring Pharrell, 2006)
'Sex 'n' Money' (Paul Oakenfold featuring Pharrell, 2006)
'Give It Up' (Twista featuring Pharrell, 2007)
'Blue Magic' (Jay-Z featuring Pharrell, 2007)
'I Know' (Jay-Z featuring Pharrell, 2008)
'Zock On!' (Teriyaki Boyz featuring Busta Rhymes and Pharrell, 2008)
'Universal Mind Control' (Common featuring Pharrell, 2008)
'Announcement' (Common featuring Pharrell, 2008)
'Work That!' (Teriyaki Boyz featuring Pharrell and Chris Brown, 2009)
'Blanco' (Pitbull featuring Pharrell, 2009)
'I'm Good' (Clipse featuring Pharrell, 2009)
'Popular Demand (Popeyes)'(Clipse featuring Cam'ron and Pharrell, 2009)
'ADD SUV' (Uffie featuring Pharrell, 2010)
'One (Your Name)' (Swedish House Mafia featuring Pharrell, 2010)
'Here Ye, Hear Ye' (T.I. featuring Pharrell, 2011)
'Celebrate' (Mika featuring Pharrell, 2012)
'Blurred Lines' (Robin Thicke featuring T.I. and Pharrell, 2013)
'Get Lucky' (Daft Punk featuring Pharrell, 2013)
'Feds Watching' (2 Chainz featuring Pharrell, 2013)
'Get Like Me' (Nelly featuring Nicki Minaj and Pharrell, 2013)
'Lose Yourself to Dance' (Daft Punk featuring Pharrell, 2013)
'ATM Jam' (Azealia Banks featuring Pharrell, 2013)

'Move That Dope' (Future featuring Pharrell, Pusha T and Casino, 2014)
'Aerosol Can' (Major Lazer featuring Pharrell Williams, 2014)
'Paperwork' (T.I. featuring Pharrell, 2014)
'Finna Get Loose'(Puff Daddy featuring Pharrell, 2015)
'WTF (Where They From)' (Missy Elliott featuring Pharrell, 2015)
'Dream Bigger' (Axwell Λ Ingrosso featuring Pharrell, 2015)

FILM

AS SONGWRITER AND COLLABORATOR

Despicable Me (Soundtrack, 2010)
Despicable Me 2 (Soundtrack, 2013)
The Amazing Spiderman 2 (Soundtrack, 2014)
The SpongeBob Movie: Sponge Out of Water (Soundtrack, 2015)

BOOKS

Pharrell: Places and Spaces I've Been (2012)
Happy! (2015)

PICTURE CREDITS

The publishers would like to thank the following sources for their kind permission to reproduce the pictures in the plate section of this book.

In order of appearance:

Kevin Mazur/WireImage, Tom Oldham/REX/Shutterstock, L. Cohen/WireImage, UPPA/Photoshot, Scott Gries/ImageDirect/Getty Images, Estevan Oriol/Getty Images, Startraks Photo/REX/Shutterstock, Jim Smeal/BEI/REX/Shutterstock, Dimitrios Kambouris/Getty Images for Nickelodeon, Kevin Mazur/WireImage, Neil Rasmus/BFANYC.com/REX/Shutterstock, Vincent Sandoval/WireImage

Every effort has been made to acknowledge correctly and contact the source and/or copyright holder of each picture and Carlton Books Limited apologises for any unintentional errors or omissions that will be corrected in future editions of this book.